Glories and Virtues
of Mary

Glories and Virtues of Mary

BY

Very Rev. J. Alberione, S.S.P., S.T.D.

Translation by

Hilda Calabro, M.A.

ST. PAUL EDITIONS

IMPRIMATUR:

✠ **RICHARD CARDINAL CUSHING**

Library of Congress Catalog Card Number: 59-28493

ISBN 0-8198-3017-8 cloth
      0-8198-3018-6 paper

Printed in U.S.A. by the Daughters of St. Paul
50 St. Paul's Ave., Boston MA 02130

The Daughters of St. Paul are an international congregation of
religious women serving the Church with the communications
media.

Acknowledgments

Quotations from the New Testament are taken from the Confraternity of Christian Doctrine edition, 1947. Quotations from the Old Testament are from the Douay version.

CONTENTS

PART III — DEVOTION TO MARY

INVITATION

And in the multitude of the elect she shall have praise, and among the blessed she shall be blessed, saying: I came out of the mouth of the Most High, the first born before all creatures: I made that in the heavens there should rise light that never faileth, and as a cloud I covered all the earth: I dwelt in the highest places, and my throne is in a pillar of a cloud (Ecclus. 24: 4-7).

Praising the Virgin Mother.—Make me worthy of praising you, oh Holy Virgin.

Praising Mary means:

imitating God the Father, Who created her the loftiest of creatures;

imitating Jesus Christ, Who had the most reverent filial affection for her;

imitating the Holy Spirit, Who shed the most singular gifts of grace and glory upon her.

Praising Mary is man's duty. Poetry, architecture, painting, sculpture and music sing of her glories. It is a Christian's duty, because from her came Jesus Christ, the Source of life and grace. It is a Catholic's duty, because the Church consecrates to her beautiful festivities, solemn functions and devout prayers.

Praising Mary is gratitude and love because she has co-redeemed and accepted us as children. It is a necessary condition, for Mary is the Mediatrix of graces and we are such lowly creatures. It is an instinct of our heart which seeks comfort, peace and paradise; Mary is our hope.

Preaching Mary.—Love is restrained with difficulty. Thus love of Mary is very scarce in those who rarely speak of her or think little of making her loved. The truly devout pray to her anywhere; they speak or write about her at every opportunity; through word or example they encourage all to love her.

Let us harken to the Doctors of the Church. Saint Bonaventure affirms, "Those who engage in publishing Mary's praises are assured of paradise." Richard of St. Laurence says that honoring the Blessed Virgin is equivalent to attaining eternal life. In heaven the Blessed Virgin glorifies those who glorified her on earth. The Church places the words of Ecclesiasticus on Mary's lips: "They that explain me shall have life everlasting" (Ecclus. 24: 31).

From this devotion will rise the greatest fruits. St. Alphonse says that since Jesus passed through Mary in order to come into the world, all will find Jesus Christ in Mary. The saying that expresses both a doctrine and experience is well known: "Through Mary to Jesus." People who find Mary are close to the fount of graces.

Praising her worthily.—St. Paul writes: "Now the purpose of this charge is charity, from a pure heart and a good conscience, and faith unfeigned" (1 Tim. 1: 5). Thus love and praise of Mary must proceed from a pure heart, a good conscience, and a faith unfeigned.

a) From a pure heart: that is, inflamed with love for Mary and Jesus.

Filial love for Mary will give us a true love of Jesus Christ.

b) From a good conscience: Our conscience is good when our hopes are righteous. A just hope trusts in obtaining through Mary salvation and the help necessary to attain it: avoidance of sin and the practice of virtue.

c) From an unfeigned faith in the virtues which concern the Blessed Virgin. Faith in Mary is the beginning of every mercy and tranquil joy.

May praise abound.—True devotion has three acts: admiration, imitation and prayer.

a) Admiration grows in us with consideration of the great privileges, virtues and graces that God has granted to Mary.

Admiring and praising the Blessed Virgin is admiring God. "Because He that is mighty, has done great things for me" (Luke 1: 49).

b) Imitation: true children of Mary are her imitators. Love is roused among similar persons, or it renders them similar. Similarity of life, of countenance, and of attitude, marks parents and children.

c) Prayer: praying to Mary, we follow the example of the Church. The Sacred Liturgy is our guide: the Angelus three times a day; the Holy Rosary; the practice of the three Hail Marys and ejaculations; meditation and spiritual reading; Holy Communion and visits to the Blessed Sacrament; Holy Mass and the Sacraments; an abundance of prayers, hymns, and pious practices—all these constitute a host of Marian devotions.

A devotee of Mary will be saved; a great devotee of Mary will become a saint.

Let us follow Holy Mother the Church: She is not only teacher of faith and morals, but also of prayer. Whoever prays to the Blessed Virgin with the Church, in the Church, and through the Church, will obtain a lively faith and sanctity of life.

The faithful, in accordance with the spirit of the Church, consecrate the month of May to the mother of God. This practice has three aims: to increase our faith in Mary's greatness through oppor-

tune instructions and meditations, to lead us to
imitate the sublime virtues of Mary, teacher and
model in the way of sanctity, to inspire us to pray to
the Madonna, and invoke her protection in life and
in death.

St. John Damascene

St. John Damascene was born of noble parents in the
city of Damascus, from which he received the name "Damascene." He was learned in both science and religion. Although the prince of the city was a Saracen, he grew fond
of John and requested him as his first adviser.

At the time, the emperor of Constantinople was Leo III,
the Isaurian, iconoclast, and enemy of sacred images. Ardent with zeal, John wrote apologetic letters in their defense.

Then the Emperor, for vengeance, set the Prince of Damascus against John by calumniating the Saint as a secret
enemy. According to what is narrated, the prince had
John's right hand cut off and hung in the public square.

Being innocent, John sent messengers to beg the
Saracen Prince to at least return his hand; his wish was
granted. The Saint knelt before Mary's image, and amid
tears, begged her to re-attach his hand to his arm, promising that he would always use it to honor her and her
Divine Son. Then to his great amazement, he saw his hand
rejoined to his arm.

Through this miracle the Saracen Prince realized the
Saint's innocence. John afterwards retired to a monastery
where he continued to write of Mary's greatness, goodness
and power.

PART I

GLORIES OF MARY

CHAPTER I

THE IMMACULATE CONCEPTION

And a great sign appeared in heaven: a woman clothed with the sun, and the moon was under her feet, and upon her head a crown of twelve stars (Apoc. 12: 1).

In 1854, with the Constitution, "Ineffabilis Deus," Pope Pius IX defined: "From the first instant of her conception the Blessed Virgin Mary was preserved immune from original sin through the foreseen merits of Jesus Christ and through a singular grace and divine privilege; this doctrine is one of faith, as revealed, and all are obliged to believe it firmly." It is contained in Sacred Scripture and taught by the Church. It conforms with Catholic Theology. It is of supreme honor to the Blessed Virgin and is confirmed by many miracles.

❊   ❊   ❊

The Lord had created Adam and Eve in the state of grace; however, by eating of the forbidden fruit, they sinned, and the punishments threatened by God fell upon them.

Grave and meaningful are the words directed by God to the serpent, the tempter: "I will put enmities between thee and the woman, and thy seed and her seed: she shall crush thy head, and thou shalt lie in wait for her heel" (Gen. 3: 15).

Let us note: these words are from Genesis, the first book of Sacred Scriptures. It is God speaking to the men of all times; He speaks with majesty, dignity and truth. Before Him stand humiliated Adam, the unhappily fallen Eve, and the demon, the tempter. Had Adam and Eve abstained from the forbidden fruit, they would have had fortunate children. However, now the harm had been done. God, nevertheless, as Father, gives them one hope and one consolation. He says: Infernal serpent, there was a ruinous agreement between you and the woman, the proposal and the acceptance; now between you and another woman there will be a complete rupture, enmity in its entirety. It will be an enmity imposed by Me.

Through her infected blood, Eve would always give origin to infected children, her victims; but I shall interrupt her generation with a new generation over which you will have no power.

I shall set up a woman as your adversary, your enemy; He Who will be born of her will be a saint. Not only she, but also her seed will be your enemy; and you will be crushed by her. You will approach her, but you will never be able to reach either her soul or mind; in vain you will attempt drawing nigh to her heel.

Blessed be the holy and
Immaculate Conception of the
Blessed Virgin Mary, Mother of God.

Thus in Mary, God Himself placed enmity for the devil. When trying to approach her the demon failed to reach her heart, but rather had his head crushed. Mary was immaculate from the first instant of her conception. Her triumph over the serpent would not have been complete if he had held her slave even for a single moment.

✻   ✻   ✻

Mary is called by the Angel "full of grace." This fullness signifies that she was united to God during her whole life; she was never stained by sin at any time; at the moment in which she left God's creative hands she was already immaculate and holy.

The Archangel Gabriel added, "The Lord is with thee" (Luke 1: 28). The Lord is with Mary. "Thou hast found grace with God" (Luke 1: 30). Adam had lost this grace and God had expelled him from the terrestrial paradise. The Lord was no longer with him. Mary found all that Adam had lost; therefore she was not only free from Adam's guilt, which was inherited by his heirs, but she was also elevated to a supernatural order, adorned with every precious gift and made the most beautiful of creatures.

In greeting Mary St. Elizabeth said, "Blessed art thou among women, and blessed is the fruit of thy womb" (Luke 1: 42). And why? Simply because the fruit of Mary's womb is the divine Son, the promised Redeemer. According to what God had said in the terrestrial paradise, Mary is the woman predicted as the repairer of Eve's sin.

Mary was to be His Mother; thus it was appropriate for her to be immune from every sin. He could not have taken His body and blood from a sin-stained Mother, nor could He have dwelt in a tabernacle which had been inhabited by the devil.

When the dogma of the Immaculate Conception was defined, volumes were written to illustrate how the Holy Fathers and Doctors of the Church professed this truth, as did tradition, liturgy, and ancient art.

* * *

Mary was free from ignorance, for she is the seat of wisdom; free from malice, for her will was always righteous and confirmed in good; free from the incentive of sin, for she was exempt from concupiscence.

Thus the Church sings, "You are all beautiful, Mary, and original sin is not in you."

As to her body, Mary was freed from the physical consequences which presuppose the disorder of original sin, even though she was subjected to the physiological consequences connected with human nature. Thus she was exempt from illness, but subject to hunger, thirst and displeasures. Even her passage from this life was not caused by illness, but by a powerful love of God, which surpassed physical endurance.

The Office and Mass of the Immaculate Conception aim at revealing the supernatural beauty of Mary's soul at the time of its infusion into her body. These are a marvelous commentary made by the Church concerning the Archangel Gabriel's salutation extended to the future Mother of God in the words: "Hail, full of grace" (Luke 1: 28). In order to praise Mary adequately we should be animated by the same sentiments which abounded in the heavenly messenger. It is not difficult to imagine what they were. With faith the Angel adored the divine goodness which was so marked in Mary. He admired the humble girl elevated to such wondrous heights. He rejoiced at the honor of being the promulgator of the mystery of the incarnation and redemption.

The marvelous greatness of Mary Immaculate results in antiphons, hymns, and lessons of the breviary, and in the Mass. Mary's name is admirable throughout the entire world: all beautiful, spotless, clothed in light, resplendent as the sun, fascinating with the perfume of her graces. She is the glory of Jerusalem, honor and pride of the people, blessed among women, prodigy of divine power, mystical city founded at the summit of holy mountains. The same words in praise of divine Wisdom are used to exalt her.

Interior Dispositions are necessary

O all holy and spotless Virgin, you were chosen and predestined even before the creation of the world. Crushed by the weight of guilt, uncertain of his salvation, immersed in affliction, man has raised his eyes to you. You are our hope: in you and through you, the criminal finds grace, the afflicted, comfort; the abandoned, refuge; the foolish, wisdom; the sinner, pardon; the just, perseverance.

❊   ❊   ❊

In order to honor Mary Immaculate, three interior dispositions are necessary:

First: A great horror of sin. Although born in sin, we were cleansed by baptism. However, we were not freed from an inclination towards evil, from ignorance or from weakness. In order not to fall into actual sin we must always watch and pray. Thus did the saints; thus has Jesus our Master warned us.

Second: Great esteem for divine grace. It is the soul's treasure; it communicates supernatural life to us; it makes us children of God, heirs of heaven. Whoever lives in God's grace also has faith, hope and charity. He receives the gifts of the Holy Spirit and can grow daily in merit for eternal life.

Third: A deep piety, which reveals itself in the fervent reception of the sacraments of penance and communion; in devotion to the Blessed Virgin, Mother of grace, Mother of Saints and Mother of

the Church; in an ardent and active love for Jesus
Christ; in a constant effort to render the soul ever
more beautiful.

*Oh God, Who by the immaculate conception of the
Blessed Virgin Mary, prepared a worthy dwelling place
for Your Son, grant, we beseech You, that, as in foresight
of the death of Your Son, You rendered her immune from
every sin, thus through her intercession, grant us to come
to You purified.*

St. Bernardine of Siena

Having been left an orphan when still an infant,
St. Bernardine of Siena was entrusted to the care of an
aunt, who consecrated him to the Immaculate Virgin.
When he grew older he often spoke to his aunt of a person
he greatly loved and very often sought permission to visit
her. The aunt was suspicious of a dangerous affair, but
Bernardine was speaking of the venerable Queen of heaven.

In Siena, there was a fresco of Mary's Assumption on
the Camollia Gate. Bernardine was in the habit of visiting
that gracious image every day. His aunt once asked him
where the person he visited lived; Bernardine replied that
she dwelt outside of the Camollia Gate. One day his
aunt followed him secretly and to her surprise, she saw
him kneel before the Blessed Virgin in fervent prayer.

She then asked the boy, "Bernardine, I beg you, free
me from doubt, tell me who the person is that you love. . . .
You are young yet, and perhaps my advice will not be
useless to you!"

"Oh, my dear aunt," answered Bernardine smiling,
"don't worry, I go to visit the beautiful and amiable image
of the Madonna; I seek only her."

CHAPTER II

MARY, FULL OF GRACE

All you that thirst, come to the waters: and you that have no money make haste, buy, and eat: come ye, buy wine and milk without money, and without any price. Why do you spend money for that which is not bread, and your labour for that which doth not satisfy you? Hearken diligently to me, and eat that which is good (Isa. 55: 1-2).

In the bull "Ineffabilis Deus," Pope Pius IX says: "The Lord endowed Mary with such an abundance of gifts and graces, that she surpassed by far all the angels and saints; thus the Blessed Virgin has such a fullness of innocence and of sanctity that it can be found and thought of in a greater degree only in God."

St. Bernardine of Siena holds that every time the Lord elects a person to a certain office He grants him all the necessary and appropriate graces.

Let us consider: a) Mary was immune from every sin; b) her grace surpassed that of the angels and saints; c) and this was from the beginning of her existence.

* * *

The Virgin Mary was immune from every sin. It is a dogma of faith that she was free from original sin.

During her life she never fell into either mortal or venial sin. As for actual sin, the Council of Trent says that without special privileges, no one can avoid all venial sins during a lifetime; notwithstanding this, the Church maintains that the Blessed Virgin was exempt from any such sins.

The Archangel Gabriel greeted the Virgin Mary: "Hail, full of grace" (Luke 1: 28), and Pius IX comments: "With this solemn and unheard of salutation, Mary is proclaimed seat of all graces, adorned with all divine gifts, and furthermore, abyss and almost infinite treasure of such gifts."

Mary was full of grace, for there was never an instant, either at the beginning or during the course of her life, when she lacked grace.

Mary was full of grace, for she had to have all that would make her a worthy Mother of God. St. Thomas says: "The Blessed Virgin was chosen to be the Mother of God; thus without doubt, God made her fit for this office with His grace. In her there was a perfection which disposed her to be the Mother of Christ, and her sanctity consists exactly in this."

Thus in her are found the theological virtues of faith, hope and charity, in her are the seven gifts of the Holy Spirit, the eight evangelical beatitudes, the twelve fruits of the Holy Spirit, and the fullness of the fruits of the redemption. Through her all this had to pass and reach souls.

meaning of the term full of grace

Mystical Union

Mary was full of grace. She was elevated to the most sublime degree of mystical union. Through this mystical union the soul lives in intimacy with God, even though engaged in life's everyday duties.

Mary was full of grace. She was predestined over and above every creature: "From the beginning, and before the world" (Ecclus. 24: 14).

Actual grace to overcome concupiscence was given to the saints; but the Madonna was immune from concupiscence itself.

✿   ✿   ✿

The fullness of grace in Mary was such that it surpassed that of angels and saints.

The word "full" is correctly used, for graces were divided among other saints, but all graces were infused in Mary.

It is doctrine that at the moment of her blessed transit from this world, the Madonna had such a degree of grace that it surpassed the sanctity of all the angels and saints considered together. It is exactly for this reason that she is called Queen of heaven, of angels, of apostles, of martyrs, of confessors, of virgins and of all saints.

The means of spiritual progress that the Blessed Virgin had were absolutely exceptional. She had an initial degree of grace superior to every other creature; she was exempt from impediments and

temptations to which we are subject due especially to ignorance, concupiscence, and malice of
the will.

Mary's intimate family life with Jesus and
St. Joseph, the exceptional trials to which she was
submitted and her very special vocation provided
for her a wondrous increase of virtue and merit.

✿ ✿ ✿

**From the moment of her Immaculate Concep-
tion, Mary had a fullness of grace. "The Founda-
tions thereof are in the holy mountains: The Lord
loveth the gates of Sion above all the tabernacles
of Jacob"** (Ps. 86: 1-2).

St. Alphonse comments, "The beginning of
Mary's life was more elevated than the height attained by all the saints at death."

Mary's life begins where the saints' highest
summits culminate. Grace is love between God and
a soul. The Lord loves saints and angels as servants,
but He loves Mary as Mother and Queen of His
servants. Regardless of how numerous and perfect
the saints and angels are, even as a group, they
will never be able to be more than servants—whereas Mary was predestined and created Mother and
Queen. As together all the plants of the world will
never attain sensitive life, nor all the animals, intel-

Mother most pure, pray for us.

lectual life, neither will all the saints in unison be able to achieve the dignity, beauty and sanctity that Mary had at the first moment of her existence.

As regards Mary, it is a question of a superior type of grace. It was becoming that the Divine Word adorn her through whom He wished to become incarnate, with a grace corresponding to such a sublime dignity. Since such a dignity is incomparably superior to any mission conferred upon others, the Blessed Virgin had to exceed in grace all creatures, even the most elect.

Mary was exalted as the Cedar of Lebanus. As the cedar surpasses other plants in height, strength, incorruptibility, fruit and medicinal value, thus Mary, the cedar of God, surpasses other creatures in height of contemplation, in strength of spirit, in perfume of virtue, and in depth of grace.

Mary is a paradise in which God always dwells! "Paradise of delights" (St. Ephrem); "Paradise planted by the Divine Lord" (St. Athanasius); "Terrestial Paradise most holy" (St. Germaine).

Mary is the paradise of the Incarnation, inhabited by the second Adam, untrodden by the serpent: "Spiritual paradise of the Second Adam" (Liturgy of St. James). "Mary is a paradise which the serpent could not penetrate" (St. John Damascene); "Paradise from which Christ rises" (St. Andrew Jerus).

Mary is a paradise within Paradise; for her singular splendor: "A paradise of immortality" (Esichio); "A new heaven" (St. John Damascene); "Heaven in which the King shines" (St. Andrew Jerus).

Let us recite the holy Rosary often and well.

The Rosary is an easy, powerful, and common devotion. It is easy because it is composed of our religion's principal mysteries, of the Our Father and the Hail Mary.

It is powerful because the Our Father was taught by Jesus Christ, the Hail Mary was composed by the Church, and the mysteries express the fundamental truths of our religion.

It is a common devotion because it can be recited in church, at home and on the street.

Ampere

At the age of nineteen the famous writer, Frederic Ozanam, was sent by his parents to Paris to receive a university education. While there, he had the good fortune to meet the great Catholic scientist, Andrew Ampere.

"One day," relates Ozanam, "saddened and overwhelmed by trials, I entered St. Stephen's church so as to raise my spirits. The church was silent and almost vacant. Humbly kneeling before the altar was a man who seemed profoundly immersed in prayer. As I approached, I recognized Ampere. After a few moments of contemplation I withdrew, deeply moved and closer to God."

The world-famous scientist strengthened his spirit in prayer; by that shining example the young student learned how to fight against the attacks of passion.

How did the scientist pray? Absorbed in God, he held in his hands a precious and visible sign of his fervent prayer: the Rosary. So-called "strong souls" believe it to be a practice only for pious women, but it is deeply significant that the Rosary was in the hands of such a great man.

It is to Ampere's Rosary, to this unexpected evidence of faith, that Ozanam owes his return to the Faith. It is that same Ozanam, who later became a famous scientist and apologist, great in the exercise of Christian charity—the man who established the Conferences of St. Vincent de Paul, a living prodigy all over the world.

"That Rosary of Ampere," Ozanam used to say, "moved and convinced me more than a thousand sermons!"

CHAPTER III

MARY, MOTHER OF GOD

"And by my power I have trodden under my feet the hearts of all the high and low: and in these I sought rest, and I shall abide in the inheritance of the Lord. Then the Creator of all things commanded, and said to me: and He that made me, rested in my tabernacle" (Ecclus. 24:11-12).

"We avow that Mary Most Holy is the true Mother of God, for our Lord Jesus Christ, God and man, was born of her." Thus declared the Nicene Council. The Madonna was the tree of incorruptible purity which bore the fruit of universal salvation.

She is the lamb who gave the divine Lamb: "Lamb who gave birth to the Lamb that takes away the sins of the world" (St. Dionysius Aless.); "Lamb that saw her own little Lamb hung on a cross" (Joseph Inografo).

Mary was prefigured in Noe's Ark, for just as Noe's Ark preserved the seed needed to populate the earth after the flood, so too Mary preserved and begot the new seed of supernatural life: Jesus Christ.

* * *

Mary was destined to give Jesus to the world. This is the reason for all her greatness, because all privileges, graces and gifts were granted to her that she might be worthy of the dignity of Mother of God.

This truth was always maintained and preached by the Church without opposition until Nestorius, the wretched patriarch of Constantinople, through temerity obstinately denied Mary's divine Motherhood. He taught that there are two persons in Jesus Christ: the human and the divine. According to him Mary was only Mother of the human person. Thus he rejected the privilege which is fundamental to all Mary's privileges.

The Church rebelled: the error was ruinous and the propaganda through both spoken and written word was most intense. Mary had prepared her own defender: St. Cyril, patriarch of Alexandria. He strongly combatted Nestorius in his stormy "Anathemas." His are the lessons found in the office of the Queen of Apostles, which emphasize Mary's goodness and call her "Shield of the orthodox faith."

Nestorius persisted in his error, and in the year 432 the third ecumenical council was convened at Ephesus. At it St. Cyril was delegated to preside by Pope Celestine. Both the bishops of the council and the people of Ephesus awaited definition of the dogma with devout anxiety. The council defined as a dogma of Catholic faith that the Most Holy Virgin is called and is truly the Mother of God. The doors of the council's assembly hall were flung open late at night, and to a pressing throng was announced the definition of Catholic truth, and the condemnation of Nestorius. Voices then joined in singing, "Hail, O perpetual Virgin, you have always crushed all heresies throughout the world." The ovation was great and endless. Throughout the entire city an immense torch-light procession was formed, and the Fathers of the council were triumphantly accompanied to their lodgings.

The heresy was conquered. No longer did anyone dare deny Mary the privilege of being God's Mother. The second part was then added to the Angelic Salutation: "Holy Mary, Mother of God, pray for us sinners."

Nestorius was exiled and ended his days in misery. St. Cyril, calumniated by the followers of Nestorius, suffered imprisonment in honor of Mary; but the triumph of the dogma of Mary's divine maternity was assured.

❊   ❊   ❊

The Archangel Gabriel said to Mary: "You have found grace with God; from you will be born the Holy One, the Son of God. The Holy Spirit will descend upon you; the virtue of the Most High will overshadow you. Just as you will become a mother in a miraculous way, so too will your relative, Elizabeth, become a mother in her advanced age."

Mary pronounced her fiat. At that moment she became the Mother of Jesus. "New pyx of inexhaustible balm," says St. Andrew of Crete. Mary is called "pyx of gold" by St. Albertus Magnus. Therefore, when visited by her, Elizabeth, enlightened by the Holy Spirit, understood the great mystery and exclaimed, "And how have I deserved that the Mother of my Lord should come to me?" (Luke 1: 43).

Having come to Bethlehem, the Magi had the ineffable joy of finding the Messias as the Gospel says, "And entering the house, they found the Child with Mary, His Mother" (Matt. 2: 11). At the age of twelve when Jesus was lost and found in the temple the Madonna asked Him, "Son, why hast Thou done so to us?" (Luke 2: 48).

St. Paul's words are decisive, concise and very clear: "God sent His Son, born of a woman" (Gal. 4:4).

Thus in the Holy Liturgy the Church prays: "Holy Mary, Mother of God, pray for us sinners, now and at the hour of our death."

❊   ❊   ❊

Certainly the dignity of the Mother of God astonishes us, not because of its possibility, but on account of its sublimity. God, Who is infinite, is the Author of every greatness bestowed upon Mary.

My Mother, my Hope, pray for us.

Thus we owe Mary:

a) a profound esteem, for she is Mother of the Creator and Lord of the universe;

b) a great respect, for God endowed her with a dignity that is almost infinite;

c) a deep love, for she gave us Jesus Who is all our strength and all our love.

* * *

Believing in Mary's greatness is our first act of homage.

St. Gabriel of the Sorrowful Mother composed for himself a **creed** on Mary's greatness.

Some of its salient points are as follows:

"I believe, oh Mary, that you are the Mother of all men ... I believe that you are our life, and, after God, the only refuge of sinners ... I believe that you are the breath of Christians, and their help, especially in death. ... By following you I shall not get lost, by praying to you I shall not despair; by walking with you I shall not fall, nor will I tire when treading behind you if you favor me ... In your name I find the same sweetness that St. Bernardine finds in the name of Jesus: joy in the heart, honey in the mouth, harmony to the ear ... I believe that you are the co-operator of our Redemption ... that all of God's graces dispensed to us pass through your hands and that no one can enter heaven without passing through you, for you are the gate of heaven ... I believe that you bring peace between God and sinners ... I believe that devotion to you is a most certain sign of eternal salvation ... I believe that your dignity is superior to that of all the saints and angels and that God alone can measure it ... I believe that God has endowed you with a supreme degree of all graces and with all general and particular gifts conferred on all creatures ... I believe that your beauty surpasses that of all men and angels ... I believe that you alone perfectly fulfilled the precept: 'You will love the Lord your God,' and that the blessed seraphim could have descended from heaven to learn from your heart how to love God."

❀   ❀   ❀

"Knowing you, oh Blessed Virgin Mary, Mother of God, is the way of immortal life; propagating your power is the way of eternal salvation" (St. Bonaventure).

My dear and sweet Mother Mary, keep me in thy holy protection, guard my mind, my heart and my senses, that I be not stained by sin.

Sanctify my thoughts, desires, words and actions, so that I may please thee and thy Jesus, my God, and gain a holy Paradise with thee. Jesus and Mary give me your most holy blessing, (Bow the head): In the name of the Father, and of the Son, and of the Holy Spirit. Amen.

St. Charles Borromeo

St. Charles Borromeo was Archbishop of Milan.

Although oppressed by many cares of the diocese, the saint recited on his knees the holy Rosary and the Office of the Blessed Virgin Mary every day.

At the vigil of every feast of the Blessed Mother, he fasted on bread and water. Morning, noon and night, rain or shine, he knelt and recited the Angelus, even if he happened to be on a public street.

He instituted the Confraternity of the Holy Rosary and ordained that a solemn procession in honor of Mary, during which the Litany of the Blessed Virgin Mary was sung, be held in every parish on the first Sunday of every month.

One night he was saying his evening prayers and the holy Rosary, when a scoundrel broke into his quarters and fired a shot at him from close range. At the sound of the shot, the prayer ceased. Astonishment and terror seized those present, and although apparently mortally wounded, the saint smiled and calmly indicated to proceed with the prayers. At their conclusion, St. Charles Borromeo rose, and to his great surprise saw the bullet, which had barely ripped his outer garment, fall at his feet. It had been miraculously arrested from killing him. All raised their voices in a hymn of praise and thanks to the Madonna for having saved their holy Pastor with a visible miracle.

CHAPTER IV

DIGNITY OF THE BLESSED VIRGIN

And they all adored the Lord, and said to her: The Lord hath blessed thee by His power, because by thee He hath brought our enemies to nought (Judith 13: 22).

Together with St. Thomas let us testify to Mary's honor: "Since the Blessed Virgin is the Mother of God, she has a dignity which is almost infinite for the same reason that God is infinite. In this respect, God could not have done anything greater, for nothing is greater than God."

❋   ❋   ❋

St. Bonaventure, Doctor of the Church, says, "The Lord could have created a more beautiful heaven, He could have made a larger world..., but He could not have created a mother greater than the Mother of God."

Everyone can understand this: even though assuming the incarnation of the Father and of the Holy Spirit, by Their choice of a mother what would we have? A mother equal to Mary, but not superior, for the Son is equal to the Father and to the Holy Spirit.

Because of this most high dignity, Mary acquired a very special relation with God. The blood of Jesus, the heart of Jesus and the body of Jesus are formed by the blood of Mary. By adoring the blood, the sacred wounds and the heart of Jesus, we adore something proceeding from Mary which was assumed by the Son of God.

All creatures proceed from the power of God from Whom they received their existence. On the other hand, Mary begot God, Who took His human nature from her. The Son of God is somewhat of a debtor to Mary.

Mary was like the arbiter of the Incarnation. The angel proposed the great mystery to her; after asking for an explanation the Madonna freely gave her consent: "Behold the handmaid of the Lord; be it done to me according to thy word" (Luke 1: 38).

Moreover, in Mary had to be found all the perfection and sanctity necessary so that she might not be unworthy of the high dignity of Mother of God.

❋   ❋   ❋

The Blessed Virgin acquired a particular relation with the Blessed Trinity.

Through her divine maternity, Mary in a certain way entered the divine family as a spouse who enters a royal home. With regard to the Father she became the first-born daughter: "I came out of the mouth of the Most High, the first-born before all

Blessed are you, O Virgin Mary
by the Lord God most high,
above all women upon the earth.

creatures" (Ecclus. 24: 5). With regard to the Son, she was a Mother; with regard to the Holy Spirit, she was a bride.

She gave great glory to the Father; indeed, He did not receive from any other pure creature so great a homage as He received from Mary. To the Son, she gave a body through which He became capable of suffering and redeeming us. To the Holy Spirit, she presented fecundity, for she became a Mother by Him.

❊   ❊   ❊

The Blessed Virgin is the true Mother of God. Thus she had a certain unique right to be obeyed by the Incarnate Son of God. Wondrous thing that a creature command the Creator! She had a certain unique right to the love which every son owes to his mother. She had a certain unique right to gratitude. Hence, at the wedding at Cana, even though Jesus Christ affirmed that His hour had not yet come, Mary requested the miracle and it was worked. St. Peter Damian says that Mary does not pray before the throne of God, but rather, commands; she is not only a handmaid, but also a Queen.

❊   ❊   ❊

St. Alphonse wrote the magnificent book, "The Glories of Mary." The famous theologian and author, Suarez, spent two hours on Mary's feast days, meditating upon her greatness. However, no one will be able to honor the Madonna as God Himself did. "And a great sign appeared in heaven: A woman clothed with the sun, and the moon was under her feet, and on her head, a crown of twelve stars" (Apoc. 12: 1).

Glory to God! Glory to the Mother of God!

The Lord wanted to save the world through the Incarnation of His Son, and to Him He gave the Most Blessed Virgin as Mother. Thus He united the Madonna to Jesus Christ, as a mother is united to her own son. The Church and all her saints, guided by the Spirit of God, never separate Jesus Christ from Mary. The shepherds and the Magi found the Child with Mary His Mother. Mary is the stem; Jesus Christ, the flower. Mary is the plant; Jesus Christ, the blessed fruit. Jesus is the vertex of Christianity; Mary, the ladder. The fruit of devotion to Mary is devotion to Jesus Christ. "The sun follows the dawn: From you has risen the Sun of Justice, Jesus Christ" (Liturgy: Mary's Nativity). The branch bears the blossom: "And there shall come forth a rod out of the root of Jesse, and a flower shall rise up out of his root" (Isa. 11: 1).

He who has little devotion to Mary, has little love for Jesus. He who has great devotion to Mary, has great love for Jesus.

Veneration of and devotion to the Mother of God are certain signs of predestination: whoever serves and honors Mary, serves and honors Jesus Christ. Whoever prays to Mary, prays to Jesus.

Mary is the Guide, Queen, Mother and Protectress of the elect. Her true servants flee from sin and walk faithfully along the path of virtue. Therefore, happy and blessed are they who fervently love and venerate Mary.

I am all Yours and all that I possess I offer to You, my most amiable Jesus, through Mary, Your Most holy Mother.

Great Devotees of the Rosary

St. Louis IX, King of France, recited the Rosary even while leading his army in time of war.

St. John Berchmans died clutching the crucifix, the rosary, and the rules of his order. "These were the three things dearest to me during my life," he kept saying, "with these I die happily."

St. Philip Neri walked the streets of Rome with the Rosary in his hand; he sought out wayward souls and by means of the Rosary inspired them to repent.

Emperor Charles V would never listen to problems of war until he had first completed his daily recitation of the holy Rosary.

So did Louis XIV, King of France, follow this practice. One day the ambassadors of the King of England found him reciting the Rosary, and he asked their permission to complete its recitation. "This is a practice," he said, "that was taught to me by my Queen Mother and I would grieve deeply if I were to miss it a single day of my life."

Emmanuele Filiberto of Savoy deemed it an honor to recite the Rosary publicly with the people in the Dominican church at Turin.

During the long years of her imprisonment, the unhappy Queen, Mary Stuart, found strength and consolation in the recitation of the holy Rosary.

With the holy Rosary Daniel O'Connell saved Ireland from England's oppression.

Garcia Moreno, Alessandro Manzoni, Contardo Ferrini, Silvio Pellico, Frederic Ozanam, Andrew Ampére and many other great men were faithful to the devout recitation of the holy Rosary.

CHAPTER V

VIRGINITY OF MARY MOST HOLY

And the temple of God in heaven was opened: and there was seen the ark of His covenant in His temple (Apoc. 11: 19).

The Madonna always remained a Virgin, and in a manner as admirable as it was singular, because her perpetual virginity was joined with her divine maternity. The third Lateran Council declares excommunicated anyone who does not hold this dogma of faith. St. Leo the Great wrote: "The eternal Son of the Father was born of the Holy Spirit and of the Blessed Virgin Mary. . . . In fact He was conceived by the Holy Spirit in the womb of Mary, who as a virgin conceived Him, and as a virgin gave birth to Him."

✿   ✿   ✿

Mary was a virgin before becoming a Mother. St. Epifanius wrote: "When was there ever anyone who dared utter the name of Mary without adding the qualification of Virgin? Such an addition indicates the splendor of Mary's virtue. Mary is called virgin and this title will never be changed; in fact, she remained absolutely pure."

— 54 —

When Jerusalem was being besieged by King Rasin and by Phacee, King of Israel, the Lord sent the prophet Isaias to Achaz, King of Jerusalem, to assure him that the besiegers would not be victorious. Since He wanted Achaz to be convinced of this, He offered him a sign. Therefore Isaias said to him:

"Ask thee a sign of the Lord thy God, either unto the depth of hell, or unto the height above. And Achaz said: I will not ask, and I will not tempt the Lord. And Isaias said: Hear ye therefore, O house of David: . . . the Lord Himself shall give you a sign. Behold a virgin shall conceive, and bear a son, and He will be called Emmanuel" (Isa. 7: 10-14). The Lord meant: You did not want to ask for a sign, and I will give you one which is the greatest of all signs; you did not want to ask God for help, but I will announce to you God Himself as help. You were lazy in calling, but the Lord will call from the Virgin's womb the Word Who will save every nation: the Virgin shall conceive and bear a Son Whose name will be Emmanuel.

This passage undoubtedly refers to Mary. In fact, in his Gospel, St. Matthew relates how Mary had conceived by the Holy Spirit and he adds: "Now all this came to pass that what was spoken by the Lord to the prophets might be fulfilled: Behold the virgin shall be with child, and shall bring forth a son, and they shall call His name Emmanuel, which being interpreted is, God with us" (Matt. 1: 22-23).

St. Luke says, "The Angel Gabriel was sent from God into a city of Galilee called Nazareth, to a virgin espoused to a man whose name was Joseph, of the house of David; and the virgin's name was Mary" (Luke 1: 26-27).

St. Matthew says, "When Mary His Mother had been betrothed to Joseph, before they came together, she was found to be with child by the Holy Spirit" (Matt. 1: 18).

Mary said to the angel, "How shall this happen, since I do not know man?" (Luke 1: 34). The Lord wanted it made clear that He had nothing in common with sin. He came to us in an extraordinary manner: the way of the Holy Spirit and of virginity.

✻   ✻   ✻

Mary remained a virgin in giving birth to Jesus. The Virgin will conceive and bear a Son: this is called a prodigy.

The Fathers of the Church apply the words of Ezechiel to Mary: "This gate shall be shut, it shall not be opened, and no man shall pass through it: because the Lord the God of Israel hath entered in by it, and it shall be shut for the prince. The prince himself shall sit in it" (Ezech. 44: 2). St. Jerome comments: "This closed door through which only the Lord has entered symbolizes, according to ancient writers, the Virgin Mary."

O Mary, Virgin Mother of God,
pray to Jesus for me.

The Fathers of the Church say that Mary's virginity is also symbolized by the enclosed garden, the sealed-up fountain and the sepulchre from which the Lord rose without breaking the seals or rolling back the stone.

In a prayer to the Madonna, St. Ephrem says, "O my Virgin Lady, Immaculate Mother of God, my most glorious lady, my greatest benefactress, loftier than the heavens, purer than the sun's most resplendent rays...; you really appeared as the rod of Aaron whose flower was your Son, our true Christ, my God, and my Creator. You gave birth preserving your virginity before, during and after your delivery."

✻   ✻   ✻

Mary was also a virgin for the remainder of her life. St. Augustine wrote: "Some want to deny Mary's virginity after she gave birth: such a great sacrilege should not remain uncondemned."

St. Jerome wrote an entire book to prove Mary's perpetual virginity. He writes: "We believe that God was born of the Virgin. I affirm that even St. Joseph preserved his virginity through Mary; so that from a virginal matrimony would be born the virgin Son."

From such holy principles and truths, holy consequences follow:

Mary was disposed to renounce the honor of divine maternity rather than relinquish the virginity she had vowed to God. Therefore, how precious in her sight is a chaste progeny!

Ordinarily, purer mothers have children more attracted to virtue and sanctity; and, perhaps, among them, some called by God to His service. These mothers are also better able to teach through word and example, the way to lead a good life.

He who knows how to overcome the desires of the flesh, has a greater desire for heavenly goods. A pure person radiates serenity, ardent piety and the goodness of Jesus Christ and Mary.

Mary is the flowerbed of blossoming lilies.

Behold her titles: Lily among thorns (Gen. 2: 2); whitest Lily (St. Ephrem); Lily whiter than snow (St. Germaine); Lily that has Jesus as Son (St. John Damascene); incorruptible Lily (St. John Chrysostom); Lily of chastity (St. Bonaventure); Lily of virginity (St. Bernardine of Bustis).

O Mary, Virgin and Mother most holy, behold I have received your most beloved Son, Whom you conceived in your immaculate womb, begot, nursed and tenderly embraced. I humbly and lovingly offer Him to you now so that you in turn may offer Him to the Most Blessed Trinity for your glory and honor, and for my needs and those of the entire world. I beg you, therefore, O most pious Mother, to obtain for me pardon of all my sins, abundant graces to serve your Son more faithfully from now on, and lastly, the grace to praise Him with you forever in Heaven. Amen.

Saints and the Hail Mary

St. Bonaventure assures us that whoever addresses the Virgin with the Hail Mary, will in turn be blessed by Mary with some grace. St. Bernard, who was accustomed to greet Mary whenever he saw her picture, one day heard his greeting answered with the words: "Hail Bernard."

St. Alphonse de Liguori would interrupt any activity at the sound of church bells to say the Hail Mary.

St. Catherine of Siena began at the age of five to recite as many Hail Marys as the number of steps she climbed.

St. Bernard says that heaven smiles and the angels rejoice every time the Hail Mary is said with devotion.

Cesario calls the angelical salutation the voice of triumph, and St. Ephrem terms it the hymn and canticle of angels.

CHAPTER VI

MARY—CO-REDEMPTRIX, MEDIATRIX OF GRACE, OUR MOTHER

Now there were standing by the cross of Jesus, His Mother and His Mother's sister, Mary of Cleophas, and Mary Magdalene. When Jesus, therefore, saw His Mother and the disciple standing by, whom He loved, He said to His Mother, Woman, behold, thy son. Then He said to the disciple, Behold, thy Mother. And from that hour, the disciple took her into his home (John 19: 25-27).

Mary Most Holy had duties towards Jesus Christ, but she also has some with regard to us. She co-operated in the acquisition of grace for us and is therefore our co-redemptrix; she exposes our needs to God, and is therefore the mediatrix of grace; she loves us and communicates divine mercy to us, and is therefore our spiritual mother.

✦ ✦ ✦

Co-Redemptrix - Even though it was in a secondary manner, Mary did co-operate with Jesus Christ, our Redeemer, in saving us from eternal damnation.

The Virgin Mary willingly and freely gave her consent to the incarnation of the Son of God; the angel proposed divine maternity to her. Mary desired an explanation: "How shall this be done, because I know not man?" (Luke 1: 34). St. Bernardine of Siena writes, "Mary, the angel awaits a reply; we, too, are waiting for the answer of salvation, O Lady, which will free us from Adam's condemnation. Behold, our salvation is in your hands; it depends on your consent." St. Augustine says, "Answer quickly, Mary; why do you leave the world and salvation in such suspense?"

What would have become of us without this fiat of Mary, through which the great work of the incarnation was accomplished?

Furthermore, Mary was associated with her Son in His passion on Calvary: "Now there stood by the cross of Jesus, His Mother" (John 19: 25). As Mother, Mary had certain rights over her Son: she offered Him as her Son to the Divine Father for the redemption of the world. In all she was closely united to the Heart of her Son, Who willingly suffered and died.

St. Francis de Sales says, "As Eve through disobedience became the cause of her ruin and that of all her children, so Mary, obedient even to her Son's immolation, became for herself and for all mankind the cause and fount of salvation."

✤   ✤   ✤

Mediatrix of grace - In the feast of Mary, Mediatrix of all graces, the Church prays as follows: "Lord Jesus Christ, our Mediator before the Father, through Your goodness grant that whosoever turns to You to beseech Your blessings, will happily receive them through the intercession of Mary." In fact, she is the medium through which grace has come to us. She is, according to St. Bernard, "the neck through which every grace descends from the head to the members of the body."

Following the example of St. Bernard, great Doctor of Mary, St. Alphonse illustrates this truth with many proofs, all of which can be summed up thus: "This is the Will of God, that all graces that He dispenses should pass through the hands of Mary. The primary aim of this divine disposition is the glory of God. The secondary aim is to honor Mary, because of her station and dignity."

When at the marriage feast in Cana it was discovered that wine was lacking, Mary said to Jesus: "They have no wine" (John 2: 3). At first, however, His answer seemed negative: "What wouldst thou have Me do? My hour has not yet come" (John 2: 4). But the fact that the hour of Jesus had not yet come, served to show the exact greatness of Mary's power. Firmly certain that her request would be granted, Mary said to the servants: "Do whatever He tells you." (John 2: 5). The pitchers were filled with water; the water was changed into wine; Jesus Christ convinced His disciples of His divinity.

Truly inspirational is **The Glories of Mary,** a book in which St. Alphonse de Liguori quotes Saints and Doctors of the Church as proclaiming that no grace comes from heaven which does not pass through Mary's hands. St. Bernard says: "The Mediator between God and men, Jesus Christ, is faithful and powerful. But men fear His majesty; thus they need a Mediatrix close to the Mediator Himself. No better Mediatrix will be found than Mary, Mother of God," St. Jerome adds, "In Christ there was the plenitude of grace as in the Head; in Mary this plenitude is found as in the neck, through which grace passes." St. Bonaventure states, "As the moon, which stands between the sun and the earth, communicates to the earth the light it receives from the sun, so, too, Mary, who stands between God and men distributes to men the graces she receives from the divine Sun of Justice."

For this reason in the approval of Mary's Office as Mediatrix of all graces Benedict XV willed to establish an **invitatory** which would summarize the entire teaching and spirit of this feast: "Come, let us adore Christ, the Redeemer, Who wanted us to receive all graces through Mary."

How are Christians formed? Through sanctifying grace, that is, through the new life acquired in baptism, and subsequently nourished and increased by each successive grace.

In the book of Ecclesiasticus we read: "In me is all grace of the way and of the truth, in me

is all hope of life and of virtue. Come to me all
you that desire me and be filled with my fruit"
(24:25-26). Hail, O Mary, Mother of mercy, Mother
of hope and of grace. Truly admirable are you, O
Mary, and your face is full of grace.

*   *   *

Mary Our Mother—In the encyclical "Ad diem
illum," of February 2, 1904, St. Pius X says: "Is not
Mary the Mother of Christ? Thus she is also our
Mother; in fact, everyone must maintain that Jesus,
the Word made flesh, is also Savior of the human
race. Now, as God-Man, He had a physical body,
like all other men; as Redeemer of the human race,
He had a type of spiritual or mystical body, and this
is the society of those who believe in Christ." "So
we, the many, are one body in Christ" (Rom. 12: 5).
However, the Blessed Virgin did not conceive the
eternal Son of God simply that He might become
man, by assuming a human nature from her; but
that by the assumed nature He could become the
Savior of men. Hence the angel said to the shepherds: "Today a Savior has been born to you, Who
is Christ the Lord" (Luke 2: 11). Therefore in the
self-same bosom of the most pure Mother in which
Christ assumed flesh, there was added a type of
spiritual body constituted by those who were to believe in Him. Inasmuch as Mary bore the Savior, it

can be said that she also bore those whose life was contained in that of the Savior. Therefore, all we who are united with Christ and who, according to what St. Paul says, "are members of His body, made from His flesh, and from His bones" (Eph. 5: 30), are all called sons of Mary, and she is the Mother of us all. "In truth, spiritual Mother . . . but truly Mother of Christ's members, whom we are" (St. Augustine). Therefore, since the Most Blessed Virgin is the Mother of God and of men, without doubt, she makes every effort to have Christ, Head of His body, the Church (Col. 1: 18), shed on us, His members, all His gifts, especially that of recognizing Him and of living for Him (John 4: 9).

In fact there are two lives in a Christian: a natural human life and a supernatural Christian life. By virtue of the first, one is constituted man and seeks natural happiness. With regard to the second, one is constituted a Christian and aspires to a supernatural end in Jesus Christ.

If natural life comes to us from an earthly mother, supernatural life comes to us from Mary. Through her passed Jesus Christ, our Life: "I am the life" (John 14: 6); in fact Jesus Christ took from Mary His human nature, through which He suffered and obtained for us this supernatural life. And this life is not a symbolical life, but is rather the highest and the most enduring life. Thus if we call "mother" the one through whom we were born, so much more

Holy Mary, Virgin Mother of **God**,
intercede for me.

reason do we have for calling "Mother" the one through whom we were born to an immensely superior life.

Mary consented to be our Mother at the annunciation by accepting to become the Mother of Jesus. Later, on Calvary, Jesus Christ proclaimed her such. The evangelist narrates: "Now there were standing by the cross of Jesus, His Mother. . . . When Jesus, therefore, saw His Mother and the disciple standing by whom He loved, He said to His Mother, 'Woman, behold thy son.' After that, He said to the disciple, 'Behold thy Mother.' And from that hour, the disciple took her into his home" (John 19: 25-27).

St. Bernardine of Siena comments, "In John is represented all mankind, of whom Mary became Mother."

In the encyclical, "Help of the People," of September 5, 1895, Leo XIII wrote: "The mystery of Christ's exquisite charity for us is also seen clearly by the fact that in dying, He wanted to leave His own Mother to the disciple John, with His solemn testament: Behold your son (John 19: 26). In the person of St. John, according to the teachings of the Church, Christ addressed all men, primarily those who were to believe in Him. In this regard St. Anselm of Canterbury exclaims, 'What can ever be thought of as more proper than that you, O Virgin, be the Mother of those of whom Christ deigns to be Father and Brother?' She, therefore, accepted and wholeheartedly fulfilled all the duties involved in that singular and laborious role which she began in the cenacle."

O Lord, through Whose passion according to Simeon's prophecy, a sword pierced the sweetest heart of Your glorious Virgin Mother Mary, grant that, while we meditate on her sorrows, we may obtain the joyous fruit of Your passion.

St. Jerome Emiliani

St. Jerome Emiliani, founder of the religious order of the Somaschi, entered military life at an early age. Surrounded by temptations and bad examples, he soon gave himself up to licentiousness.

When called to defend the City of Venice, he fell into the hands of his enemies and was confined to a horrible prison.

Oppressed by trials and many ills, he awaited death at every instant. But, in the midst of remorse which lacerated his heart, into his mind, like a celestial vision, came a sweet picture of Mary. Filled with hope, he sought her protection, promising to visit the famous sanctuary of the Madonna near Treviso. After a few months the unfortunate youth was freed from prison. Faithful to his promise, he went to Mary's sanctuary, knelt before her altar, wept for gratitude and confessed his sins with lively contrition.

He later renounced the world, entered the religious life and with zealous activity consecrated all his energy to the Christian education of abandoned youth. He carried out his work by founding seminaries, colleges and academies, all to the advantage of society and the Church.

PART II

IMITATING MARY'S VIRTUES

CHAPTER I

MARY'S FAITH

And blessed is she who has believed, because the things promised her by the Lord shall be accomplished (Luke 1: 45).

Theological or divine virtues constitute the essential part of our sanctity. They are faith, hope and charity; however, the greatest is charity. All other Christian virtues depend on these three.

* * *

Faith is the virtue by which we firmly believe all the truths God has revealed, on the word of God revealing them, Who can neither deceive nor be deceived.

Faith is the means to draw close to God. "He who comes to God must believe that God exists and is a rewarder to those who seek Him" (Heb. 11: 6).

Faith is infused in us by God at Baptism. Thus it is purely His gift. St. Paul writes: "Not that we are sufficient of ourselves to think anything, as from ourselves: but our sufficiency is from God" (2 Cor. 3: 5). Faith is the greatest wealth on earth. St. Louis, King of France, placed more value on the Sacrament of Baptism than on the crown he wore. Someone who believes the truths as explained in a catechism is to be more greatly admired than a proud philosopher who stops at natural truths without rising to God or yielding to the doctrine of the Church.

Faith is the source of salvation: Man cannot approach God and paradise without knowing this God, his own supernatural end, and the means by which to reach it.

Faith is the foundation and root of justification. Just as a root not only sustains a tree, but also provides nourishment to produce leaves, flowers and fruit, so too, faith not only maintains spiritual life, but also nourishes it by inspiring us to make acts of hope and charity. Upon faith depend Christian perfection, the religious vocation, and apostolic zeal.

Faith is necessary not only by necessity of precept, to attain salvation, but also by necessity of means. Well known are the words of St. Paul: "Without faith it is impossible to please God" (Heb. 11: 6); and those of Jesus, "He who does not believe shall be condemned" (Mark 16: 16).

*   *   *

Mary's faith was the most perfect. The sublimest truths were proposed to her and she was prompt in accepting and constant in believing them.

The angel announced a series of prodigies and mysteries to her: the ineffable mystery of the Most

Blessed Trinity, Father, Son and Holy Spirit; the mystery of the Incarnation; the fact that she is the virgin prophesied by Isaias who was to combine loftiest motherhood with spotless virginity; the prodigy that the fruit of her womb was to be most holy and the Son of the Most High; and that He was to reign eternally. The angel proposed for her belief such great things with admirable simplicity. He submitted as sole proof the maternity of St. Elizabeth.

In wonderment St. Ambrose wrote that the Priest, Zachary, did not believe that Elizabeth, who was sterile and advanced in age, could become mother of a son. Mary, instead, believed that a virgin would conceive and give birth to God made man.

Mary believed promptly. She did not hesitate for an instant: "Behold the handmaid of the Lord; be it done to me according to thy word" (Luke 1: 38). It is true that Mary was disturbed at first by the angel's announcement, but her distress sprung solely from her love of spotless virginity and from her humility.

St. Augustine says that her readiness to believe opened heaven and drew the Eternal Word to her womb. She believed and at once set out on a trip through the mountainous country of Judea to offer her services to Elizabeth.

St. Elizabeth praised Mary for her faith, to which she attributed the fulfillment of the divine promises: "And blessed is she who has believed, because the things promised her by the Lord shall be accomplished" (Luke 1: 45).

Mary believed with constancy. Her faith when put to the test always showed itself strong and generous. It was like a rock in the midst of the sea, which even in storms remains unmoved. She believed that her Son was the Creator and Lord of the Universe though she saw Him born poor and in need of food and clothing. She believed Him to be the King of kings, when He had to fly from Herod to save His life. Finally, when she saw Him in death despised and crucified, her faith did not waver; she remained firm in her belief that He was God. Although trained in the school of miracles, the Apostle St. Peter, doubted; the Apostle St. Thomas, doubted; many others doubted. But Mary did not doubt. With constancy and generosity she adored her God in Jesus, both when He brought back the dead to life and when He hung from the cross.

We must nourish our faith:

a) **With prayer,** in order to obtain from God the light of faith and a docile will to consent to revealed truths. This is especially necessary in times of temptation against faith, in tribulations and in sorrows.

b) **With the reading of Sacred Scripture** as given to us by Holy Mother the Church. Sacred Scripture contains God's own words. If we read it with the same spirit with which it was written, God will reveal His secrets to us. Let us read it thoroughly with simplicity of heart, seeking God's spirit and His divine will. The Church wants us to read the Bible as commented by the Holy Fathers. The Bible is the bread of the soul.

c) **By listening** to the word of God and by reasoning and judging everything according to the doctrine and examples of Jesus.

Just as faith is necessary in thought and judgment, so too it is necessary in conversation.

We must work—While many seek to eradicate faith from our brethren's hearts, let us strive to fight for our faith. With such a purpose in sight, it would be useful to take part in Catholic Action, take an interest in the teaching of Christian Doctrine, cooperate in missionary pursuits, and circulate periodicals which enlighten and defend souls from the attacks of heresy.

St. Ildephonsus exhorts, "Let us imitate Mary's faith." But how can we do so? Faith is both a gift and a virtue. St. Gregory said, "He truly believes who puts what he believes into practice." This is possessing an active faith; that is, living according to faith. "My just one lives by faith" (Heb. 10: 38).

St. James wrote: "Faith without works is dead" (James 2: 26).

Let us beg the Most Blessed Virgin to obtain for us a lively faith.

Lord Jesus, our Mediator, Who deigned to make Your and our Blessed Mother the Mediatrix of all graces, grant through Your goodness, that whosoever draws nigh to You in quest of Your benefits, may rejoice in receiving them through Mary's intercession.

St. John Bosco

In May, 1869, St. John Bosco was on his way to Lanzo with a group of boys and the school band to celebrate the feast of St. Philip Neri, Patron of their school. Seven boys striken with smallpox were confined to isolated quarters. They were grieved that they would not be able to enjoy the beautiful feast. However, with faith in the Madonna's goodness, they begged Don Bosco, upon his arrival, to bless them. Since he delayed a bit, they again sent word to him to come. Hardly had he entered their room when they exclaimed, "O Don Bosco, give us your blessing!" The Saint had them recite the Hail Mary and blessed them. Certain then of God's grace the boys pointed to their clothes and asked, "Don Bosco, may we rise now?"

"Do you have faith in the Madonna?"

"Yes."

"Then, rise!"

Don Bosco then withdrew with the director of the school who later returned to visit the sick boys. All were dressed except one who doubted the cure.

"Baravalle is not sure of being cured," shouted his classmates.

Then upon the director's order the doubting boy remained in bed while the others arose and went outside to enjoy themselves. A short while after, the director found them engaged in an absorbing game with their classmates. Their pustules had disappeared.

CHAPTER II

MARY'S HOPE

And on the third day a marriage took place at Cana of Galilee, and the Mother of Jesus was there. Now Jesus too was invited to the marriage, and also His disciples. And the wine having run short, the Mother of Jesus said to Him, "They have no wine" (John 2: 1-3).

Hope is the virtue by which we firmly trust that God, Who is all-powerful and faithful to His promises, will in His mercy give us eternal happiness and the means to obtain it.

First of all we hope to attain to heaven. Tobias said: "For we are the children of saints, and look for that life which God will give to those that never change their faith from Him" (Tob. 2: 18).

St. Augustine remarked, "Will not God give us any reward? Nothing but Himself. God's reward is the self-same God." Indeed, God is the supreme good and our eternal happiness. For this very reason saints renounced the goods of the earth and desired nothing but heaven.

In the second place we hope for the graces necessary to merit eternal life through good works. Eternal life is the end; graces for good works are the means.

The measure of our hope is also the measure of graces. In order to be convinced of this it suffices to read the Gospel. Many times Jesus said to those who had recourse to Him for cures, "Faith has made thee whole: go in peace. Do you believe? If you can believe, everything is possible to you who believe. Have faith, your sins have been forgiven."

❊   ❊   ❊

Mary's hope was as great as her faith; it was high, strong and operative.

1) **High.** Hope has faith as its foundation, and the sounder faith is, the higher hope rises. As a person grows in the knowledge of God, of God's goodness, power and fidelity, his heart expands and finds comfort in hoping.

Mary's hope surpassed that of every creature. A most vivid light illumined her mind to believe; a burning desire uplifted her will to hope.

In the Blessed Virgin there was no obstacle to this beautiful virtue: no sins, no attachments to creatures, to the world, or to herself. She rose freely and calmly to God and in God she reposed.

2) **Strong.** Mary's hope was put to the most difficult tests. Even in this virtue she was to be Queen of all saints. St. Joseph, unaware of the mystery worked in her, thought of abandoning her secretly and Mary suffered because of her husband's sorrow; nevertheless, she trusted in God and remained silent. A single word from her, however,

would have sufficed to quiet all agitation and restore serenity and happiness to both of them. At the marriage feast at Cana she brought to her divine Son's attention the lack of wine and begged Him to help the newlyweds with a miracle. Jesus gave an answer that seems to be a refusal, but Mary, certain of being favored, advised the servants to do all that He would tell them.

During the passion, Mary's hope had to withstand many assaults. The angel had announced wondrous things about Jesus, but in the meantime He was the victim of His persecutors; He was dragged from one tribunal to another, condemned to death and nailed to a cross.

Nonetheless, Mary did not doubt for a moment that her Son would conquer His enemies; she was certain that He would reign in heaven and on earth and she, "hoping against hope believed" (Rom. 4:18).

Let us learn to hope always, and together with Job let us say: "Although He should kill me, I will trust in Him . . . and He shall be my Saviour" (Job 13: 15-16).

3) **Operative.** God requests co-operation from His creatures; He does not want to do miraculously what can be obtained through prayer. "Do everything that you can by yourself, as though you were not to expect anything from God," said St. Ignatius, "and trust in God for everything, as though you had done nothing."

At Bethlehem, the Blessed Virgin hoped that the Lord would have prepared a refuge, but she searched for it throughout the city until she found shelter in the destined stable. The flight into Egypt, the loss of Jesus in the temple, and the crucifixion and death of Jesus were also occasions which reveal how operative Mary's hope was.

After Jesus was buried in the sepulchre, Mary hastened His resurrection with her desires. Therefore she retired in prayer; she did not join the pious women in seaching among the dead for Him Who was living, but she firmly hoped shortly to embrace her gloriously resurrected Son.

❊   ❊   ❊

Blessed are the souls who, after having done their utmost, abandon themselves in God and await help and reward from Him alone.

The motives of hope are:

1) **God's mercy**— "Mercy shall encompass him that hopeth in the Lord" (Ps. 31: 10). God is good! He wants to be called our Father. He sacrificed His only Son for us. He wants us to inherit His paradise; He has placed innumerable means of gaining eternal life at our disposal. He has given us touching examples of His goodness in the parables of the prodigal son, of the good shepherd, of the lost sheep, in the forgiving of Magdalene, the good thief, Matthew and Peter.

Mary most sorrowful, Mother of Christians, pray for us.

2) **God is faithful to His promises.** "Ask, and it shall be given you; seek, and you shall find; knock, and it shall be opened to you" (Matt. 7: 7). Jesus Christ said: "I go to prepare a place for you" (John 14: 2). It is impossible for God to deceive us: "Heaven and earth will pass away, but My words will not pass away" (Luke 21: 33). Therefore let us pay heed to Holy Scripture: "Let us hold fast the confession of our hope without wavering, for He Who has given the promise is faithful" (Heb. 10: 23).

3) **The infinite merits of Jesus Christ.** St. Paul says: "He has reconciled you in His body of flesh through His death, to present you holy and undefiled and irreproachable before Him" (Col. 1: 22). "He Who has not spared even His own Son but has delivered Him for us all, how can He fail to grant us also all things with Him?" (Rom. 8: 32).

These are the motives of our hope.

Confide in God Who is infinitely powerful, merciful and faithful. "The Lord is my light and my salvation, whom shall I fear? The Lord is the protector of my life: of whom shall I be afraid? Whilst the wicked draw near against me, to eat my flesh. My enemies that trouble me, have themselves been weakened, and have fallen. If armies in camp should stand together against me, my heart shall not fear. If a battle should rise up against me, in this will I be confident" (Ps. 26: 1-3).

Have trust especially in adversity. St. Paul writes: "We exalt in tribulations also knowing that tribulation works out endurance, and endurance tried virtue and tried virtue hope. And hope does not disappoint, because the charity of God is poured forth in our hearts by the Holy Ghost Who has been given to us" (Rom. 5: 3-5). And still further, "But if we are sons, we are heirs also: heirs indeed of God and joint heirs with Christ, provided, however, we suffer with Him that we may also be glorified with Him. For I reckon that the sufferings of the present time are not worthy to be compared with the glory to come that will be revealed in us" (Rom. 8: 17-18). Our light and momentary tribulation produces a sublime and eternal culmination of glory for us. "I can do all things in Him Who strengthens me" (Phil. 4: 13).

Let us thus say to Mary, "Most Holy Mary, Ecclesiasticus says that you are the mother of hope. The Church says that you are hope itself. Then for whom shall I search? After Jesus, you are my entire hope: thus did St. Bernard call you, and thus do I want to call you."

Grant Your servants, O Lord, the gift of Your celestial grace, so that while the Blessed Virgin's Son was the beginning of their salvation, the solemnity of His nativity may bring an increase of peace.

St. Francis de Sales

It was before an image of Mary that St. Francis de Sales obtained freedom from one of the greatest sufferings that a soul can be afflicted with on this earth. While studying in Paris, the saint was tempted with frightful despair, because he thought that God had rejected him. This thought, which was fixed in his mind, gave him no more peace. Having fallen into a deep state of melancholy, he grew pale and very sickly.

One day, feeling that he could no longer bear this temptation, he took refuge in church and knelt before Mary's altar, where he had taken a vow of chastity a short while before. He fell with his face upon the floor, and with ardent affection and great confidence he begged Mary that if God had really rejected and destined him to hate Him eternally with the damned in hell, she at least might grant him the grace to love God for as long as he lived on earth. He shed copious tears and recited St. Bernard's prayer: "Remember, . . ." with great devotion.

The Mother of God heard him. The temptation disappeared as though by enchantment; peace returned to his soul and his heart was filled with confidence and joy.

MARY'S CHARITY

Put me as a seal upon thy heart, as a seal upon thy arm, for love is strong as death. . . . Many waters cannot quench charity, neither can the floods drown it" (Cant. 8: 6-7).

Charity is the virtue by which we love God above all things for His own sake, and our neighbor as ourselves for the love of God.

It is the most noble and meritorious virtue; it is a gift infused in us by God at Baptism together with faith and hope: "The charity of God is poured forth in our hearts by the Holy Ghost Who has been given to us" (Rom. 5: 5).

We love both God and our neighbor. These words indicate the object of charity, which is twofold, for it includes God and His infinite perfections, and our neighbor, who is the son of God. "Charity," says St. Augustine, "has two arms: with one it embraces God, with the other, our neighbor."

We read in the Holy Gospel: "A doctor of the Law, putting Him (Jesus) to the test, asked Him, 'Master, which is the great commandment in the Law?' Jesus said to him, 'Thou shalt love the Lord thy God with thy whole heart, and with thy whole soul, and with thy whole mind. This is the greatest and the first commandment. And the second is like it: Thou shalt love thy neighbor as thyself'" (Matt. 22: 35-39).

St. John adds: "In this the children of God and the children of the devil are made known. Whoever is not just is not of God, nor is he just who does not love his brother. For this is the message that you have heard from the beginning, that we should love one another; not like Cain, who was of the evil one, and killed his brother. And wherefore did he kill him? Because his own works were wicked, but his brother's just" (1 John 3: 10-12).

✿   ✿   ✿

Mary's charity was the greatest, whether considered with respect to God or to her neighbor.

With respect to God.—From the first moment of her existence Mary was inflamed with such a deep love of God that it surpassed that of the greatest saints at the end of their lives. St. Bernardine adds that it even excelled that of all the angels. St. Anselm states: "Mary's love towards God surpassed the love and sweetness of all other creatures." Mary lived on this earth, but her heart was always set on God. Then this love grew immensely in the incarnation of the Word, in the nativity of Jesus, in the flight into Egypt, in the loss and finding in the temple and in the sojourn in Nazareth. It grew in the passion and death, in the resurrection

Bless us, Mary Maiden mild, bless us too, her tender Child.

and ascension into heaven, and especially in the Holy Communions she received from St. John. Contrary to others, she did not pass from imperfection to sanctity, or from tepidity to fervor, but from a degree of ardent love to an ever more rapturous state. The ecstasies of St. Stanislaus Kostka and of the many saints who lived of love, amaze us, but all their love is just a little flame in comparison with Mary's love.

St. Bernard says: "If all creatures were other Apostle Pauls, they would never attain Mary's ecstatic love, for Paul was a vessel of election, but the Virgin was a vessel of divinity. The Blessed Virgin, for the vehemence of her love, would have died, but God sustained her." On Mary's lips the Church places the words: "Stay me up with flowers, compass me about with apples: because I languish with love" (Cant. 2: 5).

Mary's love was always constant. Her heart was like the altar upon which a fire burns both night and day. Mary did not love God like other saints with frequent acts of charity; she loved Him with a sole continual act.

With respect to one's neighbor—The love which we have for both God and neighbor spring from the same source; rather, it is but one fire with two flames. This is in accord with the teachings of St. Thomas. Therefore, whoever really loves God cannot help but love his neighbor.

Mary loves God more than all the saints, and thus immensely more than all the saints does she love men.

Her charity was also enkindled by the example set by her Son. She knew that He had descended from heaven for men; for them He had given Himself as food, for them He had died on the cross.

With utmost diligence Mary listened to all the words that were spoken by Jesus Christ; she studied all His actions and all His sentiments; and she meditated upon them so as to conform to Him in all things. "Mary kept in mind all these things, pondering them in her heart" (Luke 2: 19).

Mary Most Holy gave the greatest proof of her charity on Calvary. Love is proved by actions.

In dying for us, Jesus gave us the greatest proof of love, for: "Greater love than this no one has, that one lay down his life for his friends" (John 15: 13). By consenting to Christ's death—rather, by offering His life in expiation for our sins, Mary also gave us the greatest proof of love that she could have given us. It is not difficult to do good to others When it costs us little or nothing; it is difficult when our self-love has to suffer. Greatness of sacrifice indicates strength of love. "Love is strong as death" (Cant. 8: 6).

*   *   *

We must love God with our whole heart, with our whole soul, with our whole mind and with all our strength.

What does it mean to love God?

While we are still on earth let us fulfill this first and greatest of the precepts:

By referring everything to God, as our ultimate end; by orientating our life in His service: thus we will love God with our whole heart.

By subjecting our intellect to God and believing what He has revealed: thus we will love God with our whole mind.

By loving everything that we love in God and by referring our every affection to the love of God: thus we will love God with our whole soul.

By giving value to our words and deeds with love of God: thus we will love God with all our strength.

✿   ✿   ✿

Mary loves her God immensely and for this reason, she requires her devotees also to love Him to their utmost. St. Catherine of Siena called Mary bearer of the fire of divine love.

St. Alphonse prays thus to the Blessed Virgin: "Ah! Mary, Queen of love, the most amiable, the most loved and the most loving of all creatures: my Mother, you always burned with love of God; deign, therefore to grant me a single drop of your love. You interceded with your Son on behalf of those newlyweds who lacked wine: 'They have no wine' (John 2: 3); will you not pray for us who are bereft of love for God, and who are so much obliged to love? Say also, 'They have no love,' and obtain this love for us."

St. Gregory Nazianzen says that there is no more effective way for us to obtain Mary's love than by showing charity to our neighbor.

God and Mary will treat us charitably according to the charitableness we have for our neighbor. "For with what measure you measure, it shall be measured to you" (Luke 6: 38).

Oh most Blessed Virgin, Mother of fair love, grant us a heart like unto yours!

Omnipotent and Eternal God, Who prepared a worthy dwelling place for the Holy Spirit in Mary's heart, deign that, by commemorating the feast of her most pure heart, we may live according to Your heart.

St. Therese of the Child Jesus

St. Therese of the Child Jesus greatly loved Mary. "I love her so," she would say, "and if I were a priest how well I would speak of her!" Then she would add, "Mary prefers to be imitated rather than admired." St. Therese imitated her to the point of reaching a high degree of sanctity.

Whoever loves Mary profoundly and imitates her virtues will become a saint.

CHAPTER IV

MARY'S PRUDENCE

My son, attend to my wisdom, and incline thy ear to my prudence. That thou mayest keep thoughts, and thy lips may preserve instruction (Prov. 5: 1-2).

Virtue is the habit of doing good.

There are four virtues which are called cardinal. Upon these as upon four hinges hangs our whole moral life.

In the Book of Wisdom we read: "She teacheth temperance, and prudence, and justice, and fortitude, which are such things as men can have nothing more profitable in life" (Wisd. 8: 7).

All other moral virtues can be summed up in these four virtues.

Prudence is the first of the cardinal virtues. According to St. Thomas it is the right way of carrying out all activities in preparation for eternal life; it is wise moderation.

Prudence has three operations. First it ponders the means, the end and the circumstances, then with calm judgment it chooses what is suitable, and finally it moves to efficacious action the powers of soul and body.

Thus prudence is a guide for every virtue. St. Anthony the Abbot said that prudence is the mother, the guardian and the moderator of all virtues.

In general, the prudence of the saints consists in knowing God, our eternal happiness, and ordering the present life in preparation for eternity. Prudence of the flesh, which in God's eyes is blind stupidity, simply considers earthly life without a thought of eternity. Saints are the most prudent creatures: "Be wise as serpents," says Jesus Christ (Matt. 10: 16).

We read in Sacred Scripture: "Blessed is the man that findeth wisdom and is rich in prudence: The purchasing thereof is better than the merchandise of silver, and her fruit than the chiefest and purest gold" (Prov. 3: 13-14). "And He taught me, and said: Let thy heart receive My words, keep My commandments, and thou shalt live. Get wisdom, get prudence: forget not, neither decline from the words of My mouth. Forsake her not, and she shall keep thee: love her, and she shall preserve thee. The beginning of wisdom, get wisdom, and with all thy possession purchase prudence. Take hold on her, and she shall exalt thee: thou shalt be glorified by her, when thou shalt embrace her. She shall give to thy head increase of graces, and protect thee with a noble crown" (Prov. 4: 4-9).

*　*　*

The Madonna showed herself to be the Virgin most prudent in the annunciation, in her exterior conduct, and in every circumstance of her life.

At the annunciation she revealed admirable prudence. The archangel Gabriel appeared to Mary and greeted her with ineffable praise: " 'Hail, full of grace, the Lord is with thee. Blessed art thou among women.' When she had heard him she was troubled at his word, and kept pondering what manner of greeting this might be. And the angel said to her, 'Do not be afraid, Mary, for thou hast found grace with God. Behold, thou shalt conceive in thy womb and shalt bring forth a son; and thou shalt call His name Jesus. He shall be great, and shall be called the Son of the Most High; and the Lord God shall give Him the throne of David His father, and He shall be king over the house of Jacob forever; and of His kingdom there shall be no end.' But Mary said to the angel, 'How shall this happen, since I do not know man?' And the angel answered and said to her, 'The Holy Spirit shall come upon thee and the power of the Most High shall overshadow thee; and therefore the Holy One to be born shall be called the Son of God. And behold, Elizabeth, thy kinswoman also has conceived a son in her old age, and she who was called barren is now in her sixth month; for nothing shall be impossible with God.' But Mary said, 'Behold the handmaid of the Lord; be it done to me according to thy word' " (Luke 1: 28-38).

Mary showed admirable prudence in three ways:

1.—She did not become vain on account of such high praise, rather she was disturbed and remained perfectly humble, declaring herself a servant while she was chosen Mother of God.

2.—She had taken a vow of virginity: she was not allured by the dignity offered to her as Mother of God, but rather she quickly asked how she could observe obligations to the vow, and how she could preserve her virginal lily intact.

3.—How could she be sure that the spirit that appeared to her was God's messenger and not an illusion? She believed only after the Angel had given her a proof: that is, the prodigious event of Elizabeth's motherhood of St. John the Baptist in her old age. The scriptural golden rule states: "Beloved, do not believe every spirit, but test the spirits to see whether they are of God" (1 John 4: 1).

❋   ❋   ❋

Mary was most prudent **in her exterior conduct.** Everything in her was ordered to eternal life, love of God and her own sanctification. An imprudent person is disorderly in his affairs, thoughtless in speech, inconsiderate in his relations with others, inconstant in decisions, hasty in resolutions, without regard for God and neighbor. He is governed more by momentary impressions than by a program and by well meditated principles.

There is none of this disorder in Mary. St. John Damascene writes: "Imagine Mary in the most ordinary actions of her life: while conversing, while walking, while working, while at table, and while caring for the Infant Jesus. She is always tranquil, simple, attentive, thorough, composed and amiable."

Thus St. Ambrose says: "Mary's manner was not languishing, her gait was not licentious, her voice was not petulant; her exterior composure indicated the perfect and celestial harmony of her interior." St. Epiphanius says of her: "Mary was always affable but she spoke little and always wisely, edifying everyone who listened to her." At the marriage feast of Cana she expressed the need of the newlyweds and on their behalf asked for a miracle with words which could not have been more moderate: "They have no wine" (John 2: 3).

Excessive speech exposes one to the danger of sinning in various ways. Thus Jesus said: "But let your speech be 'Yes, yes;' 'No, no;' and whatever is beyond these comes from the evil one" (Matt. 5: 37). In Holy Scripture we read: "In the multitude of words there shall not want sin: but he that refraineth his lips is most wise" (Prov. 10: 19).

Mary was most prudent **throughout her lifetime.** Heaven was ever present in her mind; she directed every thought, sentiment, word and action toward its acquisition.

Draw us after you, holy Mother.

Behold Christ's beautiful parable: "Then will the kingdom of heaven be like ten virgins who took their lamps and went forth to meet the bridegroom and the bride. Five of them were foolish and five wise. But the five foolish, when they took their lamps, took no oil with them, while the wise did take oil in their vessels with the lamps. Then as the bridegroom was long in coming, they all became drowsy and slept. And at midnight a cry arose, 'Behold, the bridegroom is coming, go forth to meet him!' Then all those virgins arose and trimmed their lamps. And the foolish said to the wise, 'Give us some of your oil, for our lamps are going out.' The wise answered, saying, 'Lest there may not be enough for us and for you, go rather to those who sell it, and buy some for yourselves.' Now while they were gone to buy it, the bridegroom came; and those who were ready went in with him to the marriage feast, and the door was shut. Finally there came also the other virgins who said, 'Sir, sir, open the door for us!' But he answered and said, 'Amen I say to you, I do not know you.' Watch therefore, for you know neither the day nor the hour" (Matt. 25: 1-13). Leader and model of all prudent virgins, Mary is hailed by the Church as the Virgin of virgins, or Queen of virgins. If, therefore, there were prudent virgins, Mary precedes and surpasses them as a Queen. At every instant of her life she sought only God and heaven with

God's will was her sole guide. (handwritten annotation)

her whole mind, heart and all her strength. She fled from every shadow of evil; God's will was her sole guide.

Mary's image has been depicted for us in every circumstance of her life, but with her eyes either cast downward, or turned heavenward in an act of supplication and always with a modesty more heavenly than worldly. Mary's face was always serene; her glance always modest, with a modesty which elevates the soul to heavenly things. She avoided with careful study seeing and being seen, and shunned useless conversations. Solitude and reflection were her delight; nevertheless, she did not refuse to stay with her neighbor for the time required by mercy and charity.

When the blessed moment of her transit arrived, Mary was the richest in merits and the best prepared for entrance into heaven.

❋   ❋   ❋

Malice and deception are sins. "We renounce those practices which shame conceals, we avoid unscrupulous conduct, we do not corrupt the word of God; but making known the truth, we commend ourselves to every man's conscience in the sight of God" (2 Cor. 4: 2). "He who would love life, and see good days, let him refrain his tongue from evil, and his lips that they speak no deceit" (1 Peter 3: 10).

A prudent soul will also flee from: **hastiness,** through which one is exposed to the danger of rash-judging and therefore acting badly; and **inconstancy,** through which one withdraws from good resolutions without sufficient reason.

O God, Who gave us as Mother the very Mother of Your beloved Son, and Who wished that her beautiful image shine with a miraculous apparition, grant, we beg You, that by following her counsel, we may live according to Your heart and deserve to enter our celestial fatherland.

Pius VII

Bursting with pride over his victories, Napoleon I had imprisoned Pius VII, who was aged and infirm, at Savona.

It is written in sacred books, however, that the gates of hell cannot prevail against the immaculate spouse of Christ, the Catholic Church. In his heart-rending tribulations, Pius VII had the most fervent recourse to Mary, venerated in the shrine near the city of Savona under the title of Mother of Mercy. A smile of peace and triumph soon lit the Pontiff's face and it is said that he told his prison guard, "Now write to Napoleon and tell him in my name that his victories are over. His star is rapidly falling!" The Pope's words became actuality. Napoleon's armies were repeatedly defeated, and he, having been taken a prisoner by the English, was exiled on the Island of St. Helena. The Pope, on the contrary, amid the world's great ovation, triumphantly re-entered Rome on May 24, 1814, after crowning Our Lady, Mother of Mercy. He established a special feast in honor of Mary under the title of "Help of Christians."

CHAPTER V

MARY'S JUSTICE

And he shall sit refining and cleansing the silver, an
he shall purify the sons of Levi, and shall refine them as
gold, and as silver, and they shall offer sacrifices to the
Lord in justice (Mal. 3: 3).

Justice is a cardinal virtue; through it everyone
is given his due. Let us be just with all: with God,
to Whom we owe adoration and obedience; with
our neighbor, to whom we have various obligations
ranging from obedience to our parents to love of
neighbor; with ourselves, in regard to our soul as
to our body.

Sacred Scripture gives great praise to St. Joseph
when it states, "Joseph . . . being a just man" (Matt.
1: 19). These words indicate that St. Joseph fulfilled
all his duties: towards God, neighbor and himself.

We can understand this virtue by considering
an episode from the Gospel: "Then the Pharisees
went and took counsel how they might trap Him
in His talk. And they sent to Him their disciples
with the Herodians, saying, 'Master, we know that
Thou art truthful, and that Thou teachest the way
of God in truth, and that Thou carest naught for
any man; for Thou dost not regard the person of
man. Tell us, therefore, what dost Thou think: Is it

lawful to give tribute to Caesar, or not?' But Jesus, knowing their wickedness, said, 'Why do you test Me, you hypocrites? Show Me the coin of the tribute.' So they offered Him a denarius. Then Jesus said to them, 'Whose are this image and the inscription?' They said to Him, 'Caesar's.' Then He said to them, 'Render, therefore, to Caesar the things that are Caesar's, and to God, the things that are God's'" (Matt. 22: 15-21).

And Jesus Christ added: "Blessed are they who hunger and thirst for justice, for they shall be satisfied" (Matt. 5: 6).

* * *

Mary gave God the honor due Him. She gave Him the tribute of prayer. From the first moments of her existence the Blessed Virgin adored, thanked, propitiated and prayed to the Lord in a manner far superior to the angels and saints in paradise. The perfume of this incense ever increased unto eternity, wherein God receives great praise from Mary.

Mary offered her **entire being,** soul, body and life to the Lord. In fact, it is a common belief of both the Doctors and Fathers, that as a child she was led by her parents to the Temple in Jerusalem where she remained until the age of fifteen. She practised the highest perfection in God's service. It seems that the following words were written for

O Mary, make me live in God,
with God and for God.

her: "Hearken, O daughter, and see, and incline thy ear: and forget thy people and thy father's house" (Ps. 44: 11).

Mary quickly consecrated herself to God: she offered Him her will by submitting herself perfectly to those who guided her in God's name.

She consecrated her intelligence to God by willing to love the Lord with her whole mind, thinking only of God and the things that concerned His holy service, studying the psalms and meditating on Holy Scripture.

She consecrated her heart and body to God by a vow of perpetual chastity and by willing to love the Lord with her full and undivided strength.

As the days gradually passed, through both celestial and scriptural enlightenment, Mary's mind opened to the knowledge and contemplation of the mystery of the Incarnation of the Word. Her heart then burned with desire, and prayers were numberless upon her lips: "Drop down dew, ye heavens, from above, and let the clouds rain the just; let the earth be opened and bud forth a Savior."

St. Bonaventure says, "Mary was the first in mortification, the most learned in the knowledge of divine laws, the most humble, the most diligent in sacred hymns, and the most perfect in every virtue."

This was the dawning, but her earthly life progressed with ever more warmth and brightness.

Mary practised justice in every way towards her neighbor. This was first seen **with regard to her parents,** St. Joachim and St. Anne. Although still a child, Mary showed for them her tenderest gratitude and affection in a most gracious and simple manner. Her sanctity reflected in others and extinguished in them every impulse of sin. Even in present times, if one looks upon Mary's image during temptation, one's heart remains pure. Mary is the singular Virgin.

Mary was **just with St. Joseph,** her chaste spouse. The Lord had destined him for her as a comfort, defense and help. Mary bore a most holy love for him; she served him in all necessities; she consoled him in sorrow; she accompanied him to Bethlehem, Egypt, Nazareth and to the Passover in Jerusalem, with great fidelty. She was especially obedient to him in all things.

Mary fulfilled every duty of justice **with regard to her Divine Son Jesus.** She was His true Mother, since the body of Jesus was formed from her. Jesus received all the material care from her that an ordinary child would require; from her He received His entire education and formation, which as man He desired to receive; and from her He learned prayers, psalms and working habits. Mary remained with Jesus in Nazareth, she followed Him as Mother and Disciple in His public life, she assisted Him at

His death on Calvary, she arranged His body in the sepulchre, and accompanied Him to the mount of ascension.

With regard to her relatives Mary fulfilled every duty demanded by justice: she visited and served Elizabeth, she always maintained good family relations with the mother of St. James the Minor; she acted as foster Mother towards St. John, who on Calvary was left to her as a son by Jesus.

Mary fulfilled every duty of justice **with regard to the apostles:** she prayed with them and obtained the Holy Spirit; she comforted them in all their difficulties; she gave them counsel when they doubted, and animated their zeal.

Even **with her neighbors in general,** Mary fulfilled every justice, for she gave the Redeemer to the world, scattered the perfume of her lofty virtues everywhere, prayed and suffered for all during her earthly life.

* * *

Mary was just with herself. Justice requires subjecting the body to the spirit; spending the time and care that are needed for sanctification of the soul; treating the body like a good servant. Since the Blessed Virgin did not have original sin, she was endowed with the gift of integrity. Her body with all its senses, her heart with all its emotions, and even her imagination, were always ruled by reason and faith. Everything in her was orderly and harmonious; everything proceeded from right judgment according to the divine will; everything favored the highest desires and aspirations of her soul. Mary gave her soul the care, time and means necessary.

* * *

Are we just? Let us consider the virtues which concern our relations with God, our neighbor and ourselves. We can thus conveniently make an examination and the necessary resolutions.

The spirit of religion demands that we give God what is God's. There are those who boast of observing justice while they scorn external worship, and fail to respect vows, promises and the name of God.

Filial piety teaches us to give our parents and superiors their due.

Respect for authorities requires us to honor in them that very God Whom they represent.

Sincerity, by which we respect the right of others to know the truth, is also to be cultivated.

We must be grateful for benefits received, and preserve humility of heart, for everything comes from God.

One sins against justice by harming one's neighbor in his possessions, injuring his person or his honor.

Sins against Justice

Vices condemned in the first three precepts of the Decalogue are opposed to the virtue of religion; impiety, exaggerated nationalism and cosmopolitanism are opposed to piety; irreverence and disobedience are opposed to respect; falsehood, dissimulation and revelation of secrets are opposed to sincerity; ingratitude is opposed to gratitude; prodigality and avarice are opposed to liberality.

Grant Your servants, O Lord, the gift of Your celestial grace, and just as the birth of the Blessed Virgin's Son was the beginning of our salvation, so too may the votive solemnity of her visitation bring us an increase of peace.

Father Claude Fernand

Father Claude Fernand, a missionary in Japan, visited a certain village one morning and heard himself greeted by a Japanese who was beside himself with joy and said, "O Father, blessed be God! I am a Catholic and have been living in this village with my aged mother for eight years. Since we came here we have never seen a Catholic priest, but when I heard that a stranger had entered our village, I hastened to see him, thinking that it might be a missionary and I was not mistaken. It is God's providence, Father. My mother has been seriously ill for a week; I think she may die soon. And I am most disturbed with regard to her soul. Yet it is a strange thing—who would believe it? She is well aware of the fact that she is close to eternity, but she is not troubled and keeps repeating, 'Be calm, my son, do not be distressed, for I am sure that before

I die I will see a priest who will hear my confession and give me the Anointing of the Sick."

The missionary went to see the infirm woman. With joy she exclaimed, "O Father, I was expecting you, welcome, welcome! Now that you are here I shall die soon; I was certain, however, that I would not die before seeing a priest."

"How could you be so sure? Why did you have such confidence?"

"Well, Father, because every day of my life I have recited Mary's rosary to obtain the grace to receive the sacraments before dying, and the Blessed Virgin has not refused to listen to my prayers."

The missionary heard her confession, and quickly administered the Anointing of the Sick to her. Within half an hour the devout mother flew to heaven.

CHAPTER VI

MARY'S FORTITUDE

Who shall find a valiant woman? far and from the uttermost coasts is the price of her. The heart of her husband trusteth in her, and he shall have no need of spoils (Prov. 31: 10-11).

Fortitude faces without temerity and without timidity any difficulty and danger, even death, for God's service and the good of neighbor. Fortitude is firmness of soul and the condition for any virtue. Fortitude is the virtue of great souls; by itself it defends all the other virtues, guards justice, and inexorably combats all vice; it is invincible in toil, strict as to pleasures and stern as to attractions. It is salvation in perils. Conquering the flesh, opposing passion, and extinguishing delight in worldly pleasures constitute the fortitude of the just.

Jesus said, "The kingdom of heaven has been enduring violent assaults, and the violent have been seizing it by force" (Matt. 11: 12). "If anyone wishes to come after Me, let him deny himself, and take up his cross, and follow Me" (Matt. 16: 24). "One who enters a contest is not crowned unless he has competed according to the rules" (2 Tim. 2: 5).

Fortitude has three degrees:

The first degree consists in the **mortification of the passions.** Lion tamers, victorious soldiers, mountain climbers, and trans-ocean flyers are called strong, but they are stronger who dominate themselves, conquer anger, self-love and concupiscence. "The patient man is better than the valiant: and he that ruleth his spirit, than he that taketh cities" (Prov. 16: 32).

The second degree consists in **sacrificing,** when necessary, **personal liberty, reputation, and life itself for the glory of God and the good of neighbor.** Such is the fortitude practiced by the Apostle Paul. To save souls he exposed himself to any danger: "In journeyings often, in perils from floods, in perils from robbers, in perils from my own nation, in perils from the Gentiles, in perils in the city, in perils in the wilderness, in perils in the sea, in perils from false brethren" (2 Cor. 11: 26). And this is the heroic fortitude of which today's missionaries still give such marvelous proof.

The third degree consists in **tolerating suffering with a strong and unvanquished spirit.** This is the fortitude of those who accept death from the hands of God with resignation, and even more so of those who suffer martyrdom. St. Ignatius, martyr, wrote to the Romans, "May God will that I enjoy the wild beasts prepared for me. I want them to attack me ferociously. . . . I want to be torn to pieces by their fangs that I may be the wheat of God."

❄   ❄   ❄

Mary is called Queen of Martyrs, for her martyrdom was the lengthiest, most intense and most loving. However, considering Mary's suffering more in general, we may say that she experienced every sorrow; that her resignation was total; that as to magnanimity she was the greatest of creatures.

1) **Mary experienced every sorrow:** poverty, scorn and suffering always accompanied the Madonna in life. Whoever is poor has the opportunity of continuously exercising the virtue of patience. Mary was the spouse of an artisan—holy, yes, but poor. In the stable at Bethlehem, in the flight into Egypt and in the workshop at Nazareth, she sometimes suffered hunger, at other times, thirst, cold, heat, rain, wind, fatigue and all other privations known to the poor.

Even more difficult to bear is distress: Mary experienced it in Bethlehem where she was rejected by all and in all her dwelling places, for wherever she lived, she was treated as the poor. But the most humiliating disdain, insult and bitterest opposition were thrust upon her when her Son Jesus was being persecuted. Oh, how much Mary had to

O Mary, may your children persevere
in loving you!

bear as Mother of Jesus! Of how much ridicule was she made the butt! How much abuse and revilement were cast upon her!

Imagine the condition of a woman who is Mother of the Man most hated and persecuted by all classes: rich, poor, learned and ignorant! Jesus suffered much, but Mary's tender heart was also pierced by sorrow. From Simeon's prophecy to the resurrection of Jesus, she was in a sea of the most bitter and intense pain.

The Most Blessed Virgin suffered without agitation or resentment, always desiring to suffer more. She lamented not nor complained; she sought comfort in God alone. Her blessed soul was in unperturbed calm, her heart was always in peace.

Constantly before Mary's eyes were the scribes, pharisees and Jews who had led her divine Son to death with every type of torture. Nevertheless, she kept her silence, prayed for them and regarded them with love.

2) **Mary's resignation was total.** She always desired that God's Will be fulfilled in heaven and on earth.

Poverty and wealth, fatigue and rest, were all equally dear to her as expressions of God's Will.

Mary's thoughts and sentiments were in perfect conformity with God's Will.

After Christ's ascension, Mary's life on earth was one continuous exercise of resignation. Burning

with more love than all Seraphs, she had but one
ardent desire: quickly to join her Beloved in heaven.

Nevertheless, Mary persisted in a perfect and
tranquil resignation. She loved and desired, but
would not have wished to anticipate even by an
instant the Will of God.

With firm conviction that she merited nothing,
she accepted every sorrow without dismay, always
blessing God in grief and joy, in humiliation and
glory.

3) **Mary's resignation was magnanimous.** Filled
with heavenly light, instructed in Holy Scripture,
she knew that the Redeemer was "a Man of sorrows" (Isa. 53, 3) and like unto Him was to be the
Woman destined to be His Mother.

After offering their children in the temple, the
women of Israel redeemed them with a small sum
of money; filled with happiness they brought them
home always regarding them as their hope. Mary,
instead, saw in Jesus the victim that she was to
raise up to be sacrificed.

But the sacred moment in which Mary's magnanimity was to appear unique in the world was on
Calvary, when beneath the cross she witnessed her
own Son's agony.

St. Ambrose says: "I read in the Gospel that
Mary stood by the cross, but I do not read that she
wept." She stood by the cross contemplating God's
infinite goodness which led Him to offer His only

Son for the salvation of all mankind. She stood by, contemplating Christ's sorrowful and loving passion; she stood by the cross, giving the entire rising Church an example of generosity and constancy which made her Queen of all Martyrs and Co-redemptrix of humanity.

✳   ✳   ✳

Faults contrary to fortitude are, in particular, **timidity** and **temerity**.

Whoever is **timid** fears where there is no cause for fear, and fears more than necessary.

Useless fear and pusillanimity cause neglect of duties proper to one's state in life. Especially deplorable is human respect, because of which one who thinks himself strong becomes a slave of the most wicked.

A **temerarious** person wants to accomplish good when it is not advantageous, or in a way which is not advantageous.

The **fruits** of fortitude are:

a) **Magnanimity,** which inspires one to do great works for God and neighbor.

b) **Munificence,** through which, in honor of God, or for the good of Church or country, great and costly accomplishments are made, such as the construction of churches, colleges, universities, seminaries and monasteries.

c) **Patience,** which enables us to bear physical and moral suffering tranquilly for love of God and in union with Jesus Christ. We all suffer sufficiently to become saints, if we only knew how to bear our little sorrows courageously and for supernatural motives.

d) **Constancy** in doing good, without letting one's self be conquered by weariness or discouragement.

Whoever wishes to grow in fortitude should make use of the following means: prayer, confidence in God, meditation, and fidelity in little things—remembering that he who is faithful in little things is also faithful in great things, and he who is unjust in small matters is also unjust in important ones. Above all, one must have love of God. St. Paul said: "Who shall separate us from the love of Christ? Shall tribulation, or distress, or persecution, or hunger, or nakedness, or danger, or the sword? Even as it is written, 'For Thy sake we are put to death all the day long. We are regarded as sheep for the slaughter.' But in all these things we overcome because of Him Who has loved us" (Rom. 8: 35-37).

O God, Who adorned the Order of Carmel with the singular title of Your Blessed Mother Mary ever Virgin; grant that as we solemnly commemorate her feast, armed with her protection, we may attain to eternal joys.

St. Mary of Egypt

Through the work of the Blessed Virgin, a miraculous conversion occurred at Jesus Christ's tomb in Jerusalem, fifteen centuries ago.

After seventeen years of scandalous living, Mary of Egypt went to Jerusalem on the feast of the Holy Cross. Although she wished to enter the Temple of the Holy Sepulchre with the pilgrims, she felt repelled by a mysterious force. Three times she attempted, but all in vain; then she understood that the Lord was rejecting her.

Weeping bitterly, she prostrated herself before Mary's image painted above the church door and invoked help from her who is refuge of sinners.

After her prayer, she felt her soul inspired with hope; she was able to enter the church without any resistance whatsoever. Throwing herself at the foot of the Crucifix she renewed the promises she had made to Mary to repair for her sins through much penance. She then went to confession and received Holy Communion. Afterwards, Mary secluded herself on the other side of the Jordan and lived there for forty-seven years, dedicating herself to a life of prayer, work and penance.

CHAPTER VII

MARY'S TEMPERANCE

Behold a virgin shall conceive, and bear a son, and His name shall be called Emmanuel. He shall eat butter and honey, that He may know to refuse the evil, and to choose the good (Isa. 7: 14-15).

Temperance restrains passions and moderates the use of food, of sleep, of sensibility, according to right reason and according to faith.

It is a cardinal virtue. If moderation is praiseworthy in every virtue, it is especially so in the use of natural things: food, rest, pleasure.

Contributing to temperance is **modesty**, that is, the fear which St. Thomas Aquinas calls "reserve;" also **decency**, that is, decorous behavior.

The fruits of temperance are: **mortification, abstinence, sobriety, modesty** and a just **measure of rest and recreation**. Created things are good. Scripture says, in fact, "Thou waterest the hills from Thy upper rooms: the earth shall be filled with the fruit of Thy works: bringing forth grass for cattle, and herb for the service of men. That Thou mayest bring bread out of the earth: and that wine may cheer the heart of man. That he may make the face cheerful with oil: and that bread may strengthen man's heart" (Ps. 103: 13-15). The use of natural things is good; sin lies in their abuse.

Temperance also teaches modesty, that is, a proper manner of dressing, adorning one's self, walking, talking, playing, etc. "Where there is Christ there is also modesty," says St. Gregory. "Dress yourselves, speak, look and walk in a manner pleasing to God, in keeping with your dignity, and edifying to your neighbor," says St. Ambrose. St. Paul wrote to Timothy: "In like manner I wish women to be decently dressed, adorning themselves with modesty and dignity, not with braided hair or gold or pearls or expensive clothing, but with good works such as become women professing godliness" (1 Tim. 2: 9-10).

Even humility comes from temperance. It restrains the craving for grandiose things and the praise of men, by giving us a true estimation of ourselves, not an exaggerated one. It is a virtue proper to God's children.

The Blessed Virgin was temperate in food, mortified in repose, regulated in the affections and sentiments of her heart.

St. John Vianney was so temperate in eating that one wondered how he could live and work; St. Thomas Aquinas was so privileged as to be freed from the desires of the flesh; St. Charles Borromeo limited his hours of sleep to a very few. All saints knew how to regulate themselves with abstinences

Rejoice, O Virgin Mary,
you alone have put down all heresies
in the whole world.

and mortifications. Mary, however, surpassed them all as Teacher and Queen. Through the gift of integrity there was neither excess nor abuse in her; all was moderate. She ate without being concerned about the taste of food, but only and always to maintain herself in God's service. Her body rested, but her heart kept vigil with God. The sole object of her heart with all its power was the Lord; in the Lord and only in Him did she love St. Joseph, her relatives and all mankind. Never did repugnance keep her from doing her duty; never did any intemperate desire drag her to excesses.

In man there are passions, which are forces that can spur him on to good or evil, but, unfortunately, having become rebels through original sin, they often urge him on to evil. In Mary this was not so: passions were regulated and only served for good. Love was always directed towards good; hatred always turned against evil. She always desired God's kingdom and His justice; she was irreconcilably opposed to sin. She rejoiced in everything that pleased the Lord; she only feared offense to God.

Arrogance is exaggerated self-esteem and desire for glory. It puffs one up, it is conceited and delights vainly. Mary was perfectly humble; in mind, where only truth ruled; in will, which always sought God's glory alone; in dress, which was simple, decorous and modest; in action, for she served everyone, took the last place, and was always obedient.

*   *   *

Pride is the beginning of every sin; humility is the beginning of every virtue. Mary was most humble. "Just as there never was such an exalted creature," says St. Bernardine of Siena, "so, too, there was never a creature who had such a lowly opinion of herself."

Mary did not consider herself a sinner; rather she recognized her singular privileges, but she attributed them all to God's goodness, regarding herself as a poor handmaid gratuitously endowed. In her sublime song, the **Magnificat,** she speaks of none but God and herself; of God, however, to exalt Him, and of herself, to humble herself. It is as if she said: You, O Elizabeth, exalt me for the dignity I possess, but I exalt only the Lord Who has given it to me.

The humblest of all creatures keeps her treasure jealously concealed. She learns the sublime mysteries from the archangel, but because they redound to her glory they remain buried in her heart. She does not speak of them to anyone, not even to the priest Zachary, her relative; nor to Elizabeth to whom she knew God had revealed them; nor even to St. Joseph, under the most delicate circumstances, when it seemed she had every reason to speak. That was not all. When her divine Son performed wondrous miracles: fed thousands of people with a few loaves of bread, freed the possessed, cured the sick and raised the dead, Mary simply remained hidden in the crowd. However, when Jesus ascended Calvary and expired as a sinner on the cross, then Mary made herself known as Christ's Mother and assisted Him in His agony.

God shed numberless gifts upon Mary: nobility of birth, talents of spirit and perfection of body. Beauty, but without ostentation; wisdom, but without arrogance; affability, but without lightmindedness. Rising dawn, the mid-day sun, the silver moon, the most exquisite blossoms and most beautiful plants are images of Mary. Rich in interior gifts, she has: a keen mind, an upright will, no disorderly inclination, admirable attraction for virtue, imperturbable calm in emotions and manner and an affable character. Even in the midst of such a wealth of gifts, what was Mary's bearing? It was always reserved, composed and simple.

❊   ❊   ❊

Perfect exercise of temperance. Moderation teaches us not to be discouraged by opposition, nor to exalt ourselves in success. The earthly lives of the just are composed of both tribulations and consolations.

Thus was Mary's entire life. But she was always even-tempered: she suffered, but she never became discouraged by sorrow; she rejoiced in consolation, but did not exalt herself; her virtue was perfect.

Without humility it is impossible to be saved: "Amen I say to you, unless you turn and become like little children, you will not enter into the kingdom of heaven," said Jesus (Matt. 18: 3). "If you asked what road leads to truth or what virtue is principal in religion and in the following of Christ, I would answer: the first is humility. What is the second? Humility. What is the third? Humility. If you questioned me one hundred times, I would give the same answer each time. . . . Do you wish to build a great edifice that not only reaches the sky, but also the sight of God? Think first of the foundation of humility, and the higher you wish to erect the building, the deeper must you dig the foundation of humility" (St. Augustine).

Moderation in anger produces meekness. Jesus said: "Learn from Me, for I am meek and humble of heart" (Matt. 11: 29). Jesus rightly associates meekness with humility, for one cannot be practised without the other. Meekness must not be confused with weakness of character; dominating ourselves requires great strength. The truly meek not only moderate anger, but abstain from it, according to what Jesus Christ said: "But I say to you not to resist the evildoer; on the contrary, if one strike thee on the right cheek, turn to him the other also" (Matt. 5: 39).

O God, as You cast Your glance upon the humble, regarding the proud only from afar, allow Your servants

to imitate with purity of heart the humility of the always
Blessed Virgin, who for her virginity was pleasing to You,
but for her humility, merited to become Mother of Jesus.

St. Gabriel of Our Lady of Sorrows

One of the saints who greatly distinguished himself
for his devotion to Mary was St. Gabriel of Our Lady of
Sorrows. His love of Mary inspired him to strive untiringly
to rid his heart of anything that might displease her. Furthermore, his love encouraged him to imitate Mary's virtues
so as to be more acceptable to her, and to work and suffer
for her. No difficulty or sacrifice was great enough to arrest
him: he faced everything with eagerness and generosity.
"No day will pass for me," he said, "without my offering
acts of virtue to crown the virginal head of my Mother."
And in his mortification for love of the Blessed Mother, he
employed the most charming manners.

To restrain his natural curiosity, to control his feelings
and senses that they might not be occasions of distraction,
and to keep watch over the affections of his heart were his
usual exercises of mortification. The noble aim of this series
of little victories was always to please the Blessed Virgin
Mary.

St. Gabriel never denied anything to those who asked
him for the love of Mary. Even if something was not to his
liking, he did it joyfully to please his celestial Mother.
This was clearly seen during his last illness when he was
given medicine that he could not swallow. If the brother
assisting him would plead, saying, "Taste another sip for
love of the Madonna," then he would sit up quickly, com-
plying happily.

In order to please Mary he sacrificed his judgment and will by becoming docile and pliable with all with whom he associated. He learned to bear trials with joy, annoyances and temptations with courage and confidence. He strove, in other words, to imitate Jesus to the best of his ability for love of Mary.

CHAPTER VIII

MARY'S OBEDIENCE

Now it came to pass as He was saying these things, that a certain woman from the crowd lifted up her voice and said to Him, Blessed is the womb that bore Thee, and the breasts that nursed Thee. But He said, Rather blessed are they who hear the Word of God and keep it (Luke 11: 27-28).

Through obedience we give Mary the best we have: our will. Through disobedience, however, we deprive God of the greatest homage He expects from us.

Obedience is fulfilled by conformity to the divine will. This divine will is manifested through the commandments, the evangelical counsels, and the dispositions of ecclesiastical and civic superiors. It is also manifested in circumstances and events, such as sicknesses and the various seasons and changes of weather.

Obedience is required by the supreme dominion the Lord has over us as Creator, Father, Redeemer and Sanctifier. It constitutes the greatest merit, "For obedience is better than sacrifices" (1 Kings 15: 22). It is the secret for obtaining a great number of graces: "An obedient man shall speak of victory" (Prov. 21: 28).

In order to be perfect, obedience must subject the **whole** man: the mind with its judgment, the will with its generosity, the heart with its sentiments, and the body with its powers.

St. Augustine says: "Eve's disobedience was the cause of ruin, for she also induced Adam to disobey; however, through obedience Jesus became our Redeemer, and through obedience also, Mary became Co-redemptrix. This is seen in St. Paul's thought: "For just as by the disobedience of one man, the many were constituted sinners, so also by the obedience of one, the many will be constituted just" (Rom. 5: 19).

*   *   *

1) **Mary's obedience was continuous.** As a child at home she was subject to St. Anne and St. Joachim even in the most minute affairs: in eating, dressing and following the household schedule; she fulfilled everything voluntarily since she possessed understanding from the first instant of her conception.

Later in the temple, she practiced all rules and regulations so scrupulously that she was a model for her companions.

Her very marriage to St. Joseph was nothing but the effect of the most perfect obedience to God. Bound as she was to that vow of virginity, so greatly enamored of this beautiful virtue, she would never have thought of giving her hand in marriage to any man, but as soon as God made this known as His will, she quickly submitted herself and obeyed. She was subject to her husband, the head of the family, without ever contradicting his commands. Although she was greatly superior to him, because of her dignity and divine knowledge, she assented to his slightest suggestions as though she needed direction and advice. She was in charge of household duties, but carried them out only in conformity with her husband's wishes, and she deferred everything to his judgment.

"O fortunate obedience," exclaims St. John Damascene, "which repaired the harm of Eve's disobedience." Mary imitated the obedience of the Incarnate Son of God Who "humbled Himself, becoming obedient to death, even to death on a cross" (Phil. 2: 8).

2) **Mary's obedience was heroic.** When St. Joseph told her of the divine order to flee that very night into Egypt it was painful for Mary to exercise obedience. It was a sacrifice for the Blessed Virgin to undertake so long and so hazardous a journey to a pagan country opposed to the Hebrew nation. She had no time to prepare the necessities for the flight, nor did she know how long she would be away from home. Her spouse alone shared her dangers and fears which ever increased due to the darkness of the night and Herod's pursuit. Never-

You are my Mother, O Virgin Mary:
keep me safe lest I ever offend your dear Son,
and obtain for me the grace to please Him
always and in all things.

theless, Mary entrusted herself to God and willingly carried out the divine will. Mary was always prompt to obey: she retained no freedom but submitted in all things. "It is God's Will": this was the motive that lightened her work and rendered her generous in overcoming all obstacles. She obeyed even when she was not strictly obliged such as when she went to the temple for her purification. She obeyed even though it appeared to men that she needed purification like all other mothers. Mary knew that this generous act would please God; thus she performed it perfectly.

3) **Mary's obedience was simple.** She obeyed regardless of whether the commands were difficult or easy; she obeyed, subjecting her own judgment and will; and she obeyed only to please God. If in Mary's place there had been one of those souls who want to reason upon all commands, oh! how many motives and pretexts he would have found in order not to obey! The Blessed Virgin, instead, combined supreme prudence with supreme simplicity. Once she understood God's will, she fulfilled it happily and lovingly, without distress of mind, or agitation of heart, or complaint on the lips.

✿ ✿ ✿

Obedience must be **prompt, willing** and **total.** All these conditions may be reduced to one: to consider in every command only God and His authority in those who command. Then, the reason why we obey will not be because we like the command, or because the superior is holy or wise, or because we understand the motives for the command and thus see the usefulness of it—but solely because God wills it so. We will never err by obeying; on the contrary, we will acquire great merit.

St. Philip Neri said, "When things are done through obedience we do not have to account for them to the Lord, for Jesus said: 'He that hears you, hears Me; and he who rejects you, rejects Me; and he who rejects Me, rejects Him Who sent Me' (Luke 10: 16).

St. Alphonse de Liguori writes that out of love of obedience, Mary wished to give herself no other name but **handmaid**, in the great moment of the Annunciation: "Behold the handmaid of the Lord" (Luke 1: 38).

O God, Who through the fruitful virginity of the Blessed Virgin gave humanity the grace of reparation, grant that we may enjoy eternally in heaven the blessed company of her whom on earth we call Mother of grace.

St. Philip Neri

Philip Neri was born in Florence in 1515. As a child he was called good Pippo. In 1534 he went to Rome, where he founded the Congregation of the Oratory for the benefit of youth. Even in Rome he enjoyed mingling with the poor on the streets, in hospitals, in the bedrooms of the sick and in hovels, as the rich in palaces, to teach them the virtue of love, to console the afflicted and to sustain the wavering weak—with his delightful joviality and inexhaustible supply of jokes.

He often said to his penitents, "My children, be humble; sanctity requires the space of only three fingers," and while saying this he would raise his hand to his forehead to indicate that to become saints it is necessary to renounce one's judgment.

An enemy of scruples and a lover of mirth, he would jokingly exclaim, "Scruples and melancholy, keep away from my house!"

But his zeal was most outstanding in devotion to the Madonna. During his lifetime of eighty years, he was greatly devoted to her. He gave no sermon without concluding, "My children, be devoted to the Madonna; have great affection for her." From his earliest years, he addressed the Virgin with the sweet title of "My Mother."

He walked the streets of Rome with rosary in hand, calling sinful souls to penance. Numerous prodigious cures were attributed to St. Philip Neri's prayers to the Blessed Virgin.

During his last illness, he continuously repeated, "Heaven, heaven where I shall be with Jesus and Mary." And the Queen of heaven, whom he had always loved and to whom he had prayed fervently all his life, rewarded him by visiting him in his serene agony, to tell him that she would soon take him to heaven with her.

CHAPTER IX

MARY'S CHASTITY

"Behold my beloved speaketh to me: Arise, make haste, my love, my dove, my beautiful one, and come" (Cant. 2: 10).

Chastity is the virtue that restrains concupiscence of the flesh. "Conjugal chastity is good, the continence of the widow is better, but the greatest of all is perfect virginity," wrote St. Bede. For this reason St. Jerome says: "I attribute the hundredfold to the virgin, the sixtyfold to the widow and the thirtyfold to the chaste marriage." Virginity is heroic chastity by which a person denies himself even the satisfactions which would be legitimate in marriage so as to preserve his whole and undivided heart for God. Chastity has found in heaven the model it imitates on earth. It begged heaven for a way of life, for it is up there that it found the Spouse. He is the Word of God. Who would ever leave such a good after having found it?

Those who do not marry will be as the angels of God in heaven. It is the chaste who become apostles.

✿   ✿   ✿

Mary's virginity is glorious. Hebrew women considered not having children a punishment. Enlightened by God, Mary understood the precious gem of virginity, and regardless of the opinion of men, without previous example, before anyone else, she offered and consecrated to God, as a perpetual holocaust, her spotless virginity. The Holy Fathers agree that hers is the glory of having been the first to raise the candid standard of virginal purity. Therefore, St. Ambrose calls Mary "the standard-bearer of virginity."

The Blessed Virgin's chastity is miraculous. In fact, it was united to the most exalted motherhood. Her purity was a continuous oblation of her body, similar to a living host pleasing to God's eyes.

She loved this virtue and observed it so unselfishly that rather than lose it she would have renounced the dignity of being Mother of God. St. Jerome said that the angel's words promising her a God as Son were not sufficient to cause her to waver from her resolution for a moment.

If the Most Blessed Virgin gives us a ray of her light, we shall understand the sublimity of this privilege more clearly than through many reflections and discourses. After having called Mary, singular Virgin, Virgin of virgins and Queen of virgins, the Church declares that she has not sufficient expressions to exalt her: "Holy and immaculate virginity, I know not what praises to offer you."

Mary's chastity is exemplary. Every century in the Church is marked by a number of great souls

O heart most pure of the Blessed Virgin Mary,
obtain for me from Jesus a pure and humble heart.

who imitated Mary in their consecration to God with the vow of perpetual virginity, as living hosts.

Virginity frees us from three obstacles to perfection: **family ties, instability in spiritual life** and a **divided heart. Furthermore, it elevates the soul** to a life similar to that of the angels and **communicates true peace.** It also gives a clearer and deeper knowledge of God: "Blessed are the clean of heart, for they shall see God" (Matt. 5: 8).

As for the special reward reserved for virgins we shall refer to St. John's words in the Apocalypse:

"And I saw, and behold, the Lamb was standing upon Mount Sion, and with Him a hundred forty-four thousand having His name and the name of His Father written on their foreheads. And I heard a voice from heaven like a voice of many waters, and like a voice of loud thunder; and the voice that I heard was as of harpers playing on their harps. And they were singing as it were a new song before the throne, and before the four living creatures and the elders; and no one could learn the song except those hundred and forty-four thousand, who have been purchased from the earth. These are they who were not defiled with women; for they are virgins. These follow the Lamb wherever He goes. These were purchased from among men, firstfruits unto God and unto the Lamb, and in their mouth there was found no lie; they are without blemish" (Apoc. 14: 1-5).

*   *   *

St. Augustine says: "Of all the combats in
which we are engaged, the most severe are those of
chastity; its battles are of daily occurrence, and victory is rare." According to masters of the spirit there
are three ways of preserving chastity: fasting, flight
from dangers and prayer. By fasting is meant mortification, especially of the eyes, palate and repose.
Mary mortified herself in everything.

One must also **flee occasions of danger:** "He
that is aware of the snares, shall be secure" (Prov.
11: 15). Therefore, St. Philip Neri says: "In wars of
the flesh, the cowards win; that is, those who flee
occasions."

The third medium is **prayer.** In the Book of
Wisdom we read, "And as I knew that I could
not otherwise be continent, except God gave it . . .
I went to the Lord, and besought Him" (Wis. 8: 21).

*Beseechingly we entreat Your Majesty, O omnipotent
and eternal God, that as Your Only Son was presented in
the temple in the substance of our flesh, so, too, grant that
we may be presented to You with a pure soul.*

Saint Catherine Labouré

The Miraculous Medal was first coined in 1832. Its
origin is as follows: About the end of 1830, a Sister
Catherine Labouré, consecrated to the service of the poor
in a religious community in Paris, had an apparition of the
Blessed Virgin as she is ordinarily represented under the

title of the Immaculate Conception. Her arms were extended and her hands seemed to emit rays of marvelous splendor. Then Catherine heard the words, "These rays are symbols of the graces that Mary obtains for men." Surrounding the image she read the words, "O Mary, conceived without sin, pray for us who have recourse to thee." A few moments later, the image turned and on the reverse side the letter M was visible, surmounted by a cross, with the Sacred Hearts of Jesus and Mary beneath it. Catherine heard the voice say, "A medal must be coined after this model." The Miraculous Medal has spread throughout the Christian world. It has protected and cured numberless people seriously ill; it has obtained and continues to obtain many conversions.

CHAPTER X

MARY'S POVERTY

Blessed are the poor in spirit, for theirs is the kingdom of heaven (Matt. 5: 3).

Poverty in the evangelical sense is not penury of material goods; it is detachment from goods of the earth and a seeking after the goods of heaven.

The virtue of poverty can exist with scarcity as well as with abundance. St. Bernard says, "It is not poverty that is a virtue, but love of poverty." In his deep spirit of poverty St. Paul said: "I know how to live humbly and I know how to live in abundance (I have been schooled to every place and every condition), to be filled and to be hungry, to have abundance and to suffer want" (Phil. 4: 12).

Seeking Christ's kingdom and sanctity is first in importance—in fact, it is the only necessary thing. Daily work, then, and material cares will be accomplished as duties, as means of attaining eternal goods: "Lay up for yourselves treasures in heaven" (Matt. 6: 20).

Poverty has various degrees: some degrees are obligatory, others are counselled. It is a law for everyone: "In the sweat of thy face shalt thou eat bread" (Gen. 3: 19). St. Paul says: "If any man will not work, neither let him eat" (2 Thess. 3: 10). Work can be of a material, intellectual or moral nature. Even respect for others' goods is a serious natural obligation.

The first beatitude announced by Jesus Christ to the world, which was astounded at this new doctrine, is: "Blessed are the poor in spirit, for theirs is the kingdom of heaven" (Matt. 5: 3).

There are those who leave all for love of Christ, following the evangelical counsel: "If thou wilt be perfect, go, sell what thou hast, and give to the poor . . . and come, follow Me" (Matt. 19: 21).

✿   ✿   ✿

"Whoever loves the goods of the earth excessively will never become a saint," says St. Philip Neri. St. Theresa explains, "Who runs after perishable things will himself perish."

Blessed are the poor because in God they find every good; in poverty they find their paradise on earth as St. Francis did, when he exclaimed, "My God and my all." St. Augustine advised: "Love that one Good in which all good things are found." St. Ignatius prayed: "Give me only Thy love with Thy grace and I am rich enough." When poverty afflicts us let us remember that Jesus and His Mother were poor. St. Bonaventure said: "Poor one, console yourself with the thought that Jesus and His Mother were also poor like you."

Poverty is feared by pagans and even by many Christians, although they admit in theory that riches do not make men happy. Jesus Christ, instead, practiced poverty, taught its value and elevated it to the level of an evangelical counsel for men. In itself, poverty is not the principal evangelical counsel, but it is the point of departure. It is there that detachment from the world begins; poverty is the first step on the ladder towards eternal goods, towards God, infinite Good.

Thus the renunciation of riches and the true and real detachment from them is the first act that Jesus asked of the Apostles, of the young man who sought the way of perfection and of all those who want to follow Him. St. Francis of Assisi, doctor, lover and spouse of poverty, asked all those who wished to become his followers, first of all, to sell their possessions and distribute them to the poor.

The humble man conquers the proud, the chaste defeats the vicious, the poor man triumphs over the rich man and transforms him into his co-operator, because he is armed by that divine power which is inherent in poverty.

☼   ☼   ☼

Mary was poor by preference. The Blessed Virgin, illumined by the Holy Spirit, understood the secret of merit and peace hidden in poverty.

St. Peter Canisius says that Mary could have lived in comfort, on her inheritance, but for love of poverty, she preferred to remain poor, and reserving only a small portion for herself, distributed the rest in alms to the temple and the poor.

Mary was poor by reason of her detachment from all earthly goods, poor by reason of her renunciation of these, and poor by reason of the vow of povery she had made to God. At the stable in Bethlehem later, her heart became inflamed with love of the beautiful virtue of poverty. She made great progress in this virtue as she saw the Incarnate Word choose a stable for His lodging, a manger for a throne and two animals as courtiers. The most severe poverty became her delight; the rough stable and coarse wool clothing were dearer to her than a palace and luxurious robes. The Son of God was born in poverty, and as a poor man He lived and died. His most holy Mother shared His condition with a loving heart. Behold our Divine Master! Behold our Heavenly Mistress!

✿   ✿   ✿

Mary was poor in actuality. She not only lacked the comforts of life in every circumstance, but at times, even the barest necessities.

As a spouse, God gave her a man who was obliged to earn his living by the sweat of his brow.

In Bethlehem Mary found no shelter because she looked poor: "There was no room for them in the inn" (Luke 2: 7).

Grant that I may praise you,
O sacred Virgin;
Give me strength against your enemies.

Forced to leave the city, she found refuge in a barren stable that was exposed to the elements.

In Egypt, Mary lived by her own labors and the toil of her spouse. How many times she must have found herself with hardly enough to live on! How many times she must have known great want in both food and shelter!

Once she was invited to a wedding, but whose wedding? The wedding of a couple who ran out of wine at the height of the feast. One usually sends wedding invitations to those of one's own social class. Now if the host at this wedding was so poor, his guests must not have been much better off. Jesus Christ could say: "The foxes have dens, and the birds of the air have nests, but the Son of Man has nowhere to lay His head" (Luke 9: 58). If the Redeemer had no place to rest His head, could His most holy Mother be much different from Him?

❊   ❊   ❊

Mary manifested her poverty. She did not hide it; rather, she wished to appear poor and be considered so by all. After the birth of Jesus she offered a pair of turtle doves or two young pigeons in the temple; this was the customary offering of the poor. Could she not have used the gold given her by the Magi, and make the customary offering of the rich? Certainly! "But the gold," says St. Bonaventure, "passed quickly from her hands to St. Joseph's,

and from his into the hands of the poor." Left thus
in her indigence, Mary enjoyed being numbered
among the poor.

When Jesus on the cross thought of giving His
most holy Mother a support, He entrusted her to a
poor fisherman: the Apostle, St. John. He could
have entrusted her to a wealthy disciple, such as
John of Arimathea or Nicodemus. "He did not do
this," says St. Augustine, "out of consideration for
Mary's spirit and desire, for she wished to live as
the poor and as such she wished to be known."

The Apostles collected alms from the faithful
to help needy widows; Mary was not ashamed
to accept her portion. Let us see to it that her example encourages us to appear before the world with
the signs of Christ's poverty.

Greed for money, the greatest obstacle to
perfection, is removed by virtue of poverty. Riches
are occasions for many sins.

Poverty unites souls to the Lord Who says, "I
am your reward exceedingly great;" the poor man
who loves God happily exclaims, "My God and
my all!"

The theological virtues are increased by poverty; in fact, St. Ambrose calls poverty the mother
and nurse of every virtue. The Lord speaks to the
heart of the poor; He gives their souls the wisdom
of celestial truths. The poor find it easy to hope for
heaven and they desire it; they expect nothing from

this world. St. Bernard writes: "Poverty was not found in heaven, although it abounded on earth, but man was not aware of its value. For this reason, the Son of God willed to descend from heaven to show men the value of poverty. Mary embraced it faithfully and professed it."

To keep the heart detached from riches is an absolute necessity for salvation. Jesus says: "Every one of you who does not renounce all that he possesses cannot be My disciple" (Luke 14: 33). Woe to the rich! "It is easier for a camel to pass through the eye of a needle, than for a rich man to enter into the kingdom of heaven" (Matt. 19: 24).

St. Augustine said: "Riches are snares for the wings; they prevent the soul from rising to celestial things. In fact, he who has consolations on this earth forgets heaven."

Patience is necessary in distress and privation.

Poverty is always a bit humiliating: in regard to the dwelling, clothing and food; the poor are embarrased on the street, in church and in any public place. However, these humiliations are glorious. St. Paul writes: "I have suffered the loss of all things, and I count them as dung that I may gain Christ" (Phil. 3: 8).

The Divine Master said: "Make friends for yourselves with the mammon of wickedness, so that when you fail they may receive you into everlasting dwellings" (Luke 16: 9). What we give to the poor will be ours for eternity. Whoever gives to the needy receives from God.

Grant Your servants, O Lord, the gift of heavenly grace, and just as the Blessed Virgin's Son was the beginning of our salvation, so may the votive solemnity of her espousals bring us an increase of peace.

St. Peter Damian

When Peter Damian was a child he found a silver coin one day. He was a poor orphan, ill-treated by his older brother, with whom he lived. "How shall I use this money?" the child asked himself. He glanced at his patched clothing and felt the pangs of hunger, but on seeing a priest passing by, he remembered his deceased parents and made his decision. Running to the priest, he said, "Take this and please say a Mass for the repose of my poor dead parents!"

From that day on, protected by the Virgin, who was greatly pleased with his generosity, and favored by the holy souls in purgatory, Peter had a happier life. Another brother, named Damian, took him in and sent him to school; and he grew in wisdom and virtue. Upon seeing two monks of St. Romualdo one day, he went with them to Fonte Avellana and was clothed in the Camaldolese habit. He became an exemplary monk, ardently devoted to Mary. Later he was made bishop and then cardinal.

He strenuously combated heretics, brought the inhabitants of Ravenna to obedience to the Apostolic See and recalled Henry IV, Emperor of Germany, to his duty. A fervent apostle of Mary, he propagated her devotion everywhere and promoted the recitation of her office.

Peter Damian died serenely in Faenza in 1072 and was canonized by Pope Leo XII.

PART III
DEVOTION TO MARY

CHAPTER I

DEVOTION TO MARY MOST HOLY

And there shall come forth a rod out of the root of Jesse, and a flower shall rise up out of his root. And the spirit of the Lord shall rest upon him: the spirit of wisdom, and of understanding, the spirit of counsel, and of fortitude, the spirit of knowledge, and of godliness. And he shall be filled with the spirit of the fear of the Lord (Isa. 11: 1-3).

To the saints, we give a cult of dulia; to Mary, a cult of supreme dulia or hyperdulia.

Devotion to Mary is based on her highly special affinity with Jesus Christ.

As the true Mother of God, Mary entered into a special relationship with the Blessed Trinity, for reason of which she is daughter, spouse and Mother of God. Catholics profess that the distance between Mary and God is infinite, but between the Saints and Mary it is immense. To God, therefore, is given adoration; to Mary, supreme veneration; to the saints and angels, simple veneration.

❋ ❋ ❋

The cult to Mary began in the terrestrial paradise when God spoke of the woman: "I will put enmities between thee and the woman . . . she shall crush thy head" (Gen. 3: 15).

It was from that day that humanity began to hope in Mary as in the fortunate creature who would obtain revenge over the devil.

In the Old Testament, Isaias and Jeremias speak to us in detail of Mary. The most beautiful symbols are used to describe her; various types of women prefigure her: Sara, Rebecca, Rachel, Judith and Esther. She is represented by Noe's Ark, the Tabernacle of the Alliance and Jacob's ladder. "All the rich among the people shall entreat thy countenance" (Ps. 44: 13).

* * *

In the New Testament, beginning with the Apostles, signs of love, veneration and devotion were given to Mary. Numerous pictures in the catacombs illustrate this fact. This is also true of the Liturgy. For example, in the Syriac Liturgy, we read the invocation, "Holy Mary, pray for us sinners."

The Fathers and Doctors of the Church praised Mary highly in their sermons and writings—particularly St. Ephrem, St. Sophronius, St. Epiphanius, St. Andrew of Crete, St. John Damascene, St. Bernard, St. Thomas, St. Bonaventure, St. Francis de Sales and St. Alphonse de Liguori. Books concerning the Madonna would today fill immense libraries.

Feasts in honor of Mary, litanies, the months of May and October, numerous shrines, Saturday

Most high Queen of the universe,
Mary ever Virgin, make intercession
for our peace and salvation.

dedicated to Mary and the Angelus are further proofs of the sublimity of devotion to the Blessed Virgin.

Pope Leo XIII wrote twelve encyclicals on the Holy Rosary. Art always honored the Blessed Virgin: architecture, with churches and shrines; sculpture, with beautiful statues of the Madonna; painting, with innumerable pictures of Mary; music, with a variety of Marian hymns; and poets and writers, with the best of their works.

Among Christians it is known that wherever the Gospel reaches, there also will penetrate devotion to Mary; in fact, devotion to Mary often precedes the entrance of the Gospel.

There is no diocese, parish, mission or religious house without devotion to Mary; at least an altar, picture or devotional practice will always be found. Even many schismatics and heretics honor the Blessed Mother and hope in her.

Our love for Mary is joined to our love for Jesus Christ. There is no Christian who does not feel drawn to Mary.

Whoever finds Mary finds Jesus Christ.

Devotion to Mary is so closely bound up with Christian life that St. Alphonse and recent Doctors of the Church say that it is of moral necessity for our salvation. Through this devotion, faith is strengthened, charity is enkindled and the Liturgy assumes forms and manifestations both attractive and edifying.

A true devotion to Mary is a sign of a true devotion to Jesus Christ. God has united Mother and Son; let man not separate them.

All the love, trust and praise given to Mary ends in God. We praise Mary Most Holy to sing of the special gifts God gave her, in the same spirit with which Mary said: "He Who is mighty has done great things for me" (Luke 1: 49).

Let us imitate Mary Most Holy. We shall thus find the practice of virtue much easier.

Let us pray to the Blessed Virgin so that she will intercede for us to the Lord; God is much more honored by Mary's petitions than by ours.

Let us trust in Mary in order to favor the desire of God, Who wanted all graces to come to us by the hands of Mary.

Grant, we beseech You, O Lord, perpetual health of soul and body, and, through the intercession of Mary ever Virgin, free us from present sadness and admit us to eternal joy.

Mary Help of Christians

In 1683 the Turks besieged the city of Vienna. The inhabitants prayed fervently to Mary Most Holy, honored by the people of Bavaria under the title of "Madonna of Help."

Their prayers were heard: Vienna was freed from the siege.

In perpetual memory of the event, Pope Innocent XI instituted the Confraternity of Mary our Help, which became widespread throughout the world.

After a victory over Turkish fleets at Lepanto, Pius V ordained that the invocation, "Help of Christians, pray for us," be added to the litanies.

Through the efforts of St. John Bosco, a majestic church in honor of Mary, Help of Christians, was erected at Turin. The faithful come in great throngs to this church, a true shrine, where the Madonna dispenses her graces and blessings.

CHAPTER II

THE HAIL MARY—I

*And when the angel had come to her, he said to her,
'Hail, full of grace, the Lord is with thee. Blessed art thou
among women'* (Luke 1: 28).

**Hail Mary, full of grace; the Lord is with thee;
blessed art thou among women, and blessed is the
fruit of thy womb, Jesus.**

This is the most beautiful of all the prayers
directed to the Mother of God.

It is divided into two parts: the first part
can be called **praise**; the second part contains a **petition.**

The **praise** is composed of words of Holy Scripture, that is, the expressions used by the Archangel
Gabriel when announcing the mystery of the Incarnation: "Hail, full of grace, the Lord is with thee"
(Luke 1: 28), and Elizabeth's words during Mary's
visit: "Blessed art thou among women and blessed
is the fruit of thy womb" (Luke 1: 42).

These words contain in brief all the praise that
can be given to Mary.

The **petition** is composed of words of the
Church: "Holy Mary, Mother of God, pray for us
sinners, now and at the hour of our death.
Amen."

Let us now consider the first part:

1) **Hail:** It is a greeting that expresses a wish for great blessings and also congratulations for goods already possessed. Our wish is that Mary's glory increase among men; we hope for the expansion of Mary's kingdom because we want Christ's kingdom to be spread. Together with Mary we rejoice for the privileges, virtues, dignity and glory that she has received from the Blessed Trinity.

After the sin of Adam, Mary was the first human being to receive the salutation, "Peace be with you;" in fact, she was in peace and was loved by God because of her grace. Jesus Christ obtained peace, distributed it and wished it to all men.

Concerning the angelic salutation St. Thomas Aquinas says, "In the Old Testament the apparition of angels to men was in itself considered a great event, so much so, that it was deemed an honor to serve them. Thus Genesis praises Abraham for his homage and hospitality to angels. However, it was unheard of that an angel should pay tribute to man until Gabriel said, **Ave,** in his salutation to the Madonna."

This occurred because Mary was superior to the angels by reason of her dignity, her union with God and her fullness of grace.

2) **Full of Grace.** The angel did not say, "**Mary,** you who are full of grace;" but rather, he called her, the one full of grace. In fact, Mary had relative full-

To you, O Virgin Mother, who were never touched by any spot of original or actual sin, I commend and entrust the purity of my heart.

ness, which allowed for additional increase, but she was full according to her actual capacity and according to the nobility of her mission.

St. Thomas Aquinas says that the Mother of God was full of grace in three respects: in soul, body and humanity.

In soul: for Mary could, in the most perfect manner, avoid sin and practise every virtue to a heroic degree; consequently, she is called Queen of Saints.

In body: for the superabundance of grace in her was so great that it was transfused from her soul to her body, which was sanctified, so as to be a worthy tabernacle for the Son of God Incarnate. In fact, Mary had to give something of her body to the formation of Jesus Christ's sacred humanity; the grace of her soul irradiated light and beauty in her body.

In humanity: Mary had a fullness of grace for all men; she was destined to be the universal mediatrix between the Son of God and us.

Mary is symbolized by the sun which illumines the entire earth.

3) **The Lord is with thee.** The effect of the fullness of grace is union with God. God dwells in the soul that is in the state of grace. "If anyone love Me, he will keep My word, and My Father will love him and We will come to him and make Our abode with him" (John 14: 23). When the angel pronounced the words, **"The Lord is with thee,"** he was

not merely making a wish; he was affirming a fact:
If God is in every place, He is present in a special
way in the soul that is in the state of grace. This is
the indwelling of God in us. But in Mary God's indwelling takes place in a far more perfect manner
than in the saints. The Blessed Virgin possessed a
singular grace; she was loved by God more than all
the angels and saints together.

The Fathers of the Church say that the Blessed
Trinity dwells in Mary as in the most honored
abode. The Blessed Trinity penetrated Mary's whole
soul: thoughts, will, and heart. St. Bernard says to
Mary: "It is not only the Son Who is found in you,
clothed with your flesh, but also the Holy Spirit,
through Whose virtue you conceived, and the
Father, Who generated Him Whom you conceived.
With you is the Father, Who made His Son your
Son; with you is the Son, Who fulfills the admirable
mystery of the Incarnation; with you is the Holy
Spirit, Who, together with the Father and Son,
sanctifies your virginal womb."

4) **Blessed art thou among women.** God is
generous in His blessings for the saints, but with
His own Mother He is most generous. David said:
"The Lord ruleth me: and I shall want nothing" (Ps.
22: 1); thus Jesus addressed the Apostles as friends:
"You are My friends" (John 15: 14), and, according-
ly, blessed them greatly. All creatures, even though
they may be saints, are loved as servants; Mary, in-

stead, is loved as a Mother. Jesus called her with this name that made her heart leap with joy. Thus, according to St. Elizabeth's words, Mary is the pre-eminently blessed one.

In Holy Scripture maternity is considered a divine blessing, but in Mary maternity is of an order immensely superior and wholly extraordinary. Thus, St. Elizabeth said in amazement: "And how have I deserved that the Mother of my Lord should come to me?" (Luke 1: 43).

"Truly blessed," says St. Peter Chrysologus, "is she who was greater than the universe. She alone contains the One Whom the entire world cannot contain. She bore Him Who bears the world; she begot her Creator; she nourished Him Who nourishes each creature."

5) **Blessed is the fruit of thy womb, Jesus.** He is the **blessed One,** in fact, the **One Who blesses blessing itself;** and from the fullness of Jesus, Mary also received blessings; "And of His fullness we all have received, grace for grace" (John 1: 16). For this reason, seeing that Mary was so blessed, Elizabeth praised God saying: "Blessed is the fruit of thy womb!" (Luke 1: 42). Mary was **pre-eminently** blessed among God's creatures.

Jesus Christ is the blessing: a) for the angels, who according to the Apocalypse sing to Him: "Blessing and glory and wisdom and thanksgiving" (Apoc. 7: 12); b) for the Hebrews, in whose midst

He walked, sowing blessings and receiving their song: "Blessed is He Who comes in the name of the Lord!" (Matt. 21: 9); c) for all Christians, as St. Paul writes: "Blessed be the God and Father of our Lord Jesus Christ, Who has blessed us with every spiritual blessing on high in Christ" (Ephes. 1, 3).

St. Thomas Aquinas contrasts the fruit eaten by Eve and offered to Adam with the fruit borne by Mary in her womb and offered to the world. According to this holy Doctor, Eve desired three things from her fruit. Trusting in the devil's false promise she wished to become **similar to God** in the knowledge of good and evil. Instead, by sinning, she found herself far away from God and exiled from the terrestrial paradise. The fruit of Mary, on the other hand, unites us to God, rendering us similar to Him.

In the second place Eve desired **pleasure** from her fruit, which she thought would be delicious. But after eating it, she found herself immersed in shame and sorrow. Most delectable, on the contrary, is the fruit of Mary which, when eaten in the Holy Eucharist, leads us safely to the delights of eternal life.

Eve also had **dreams of beauty,** but true beauty is in Jesus, Mary's fruit, for it is written of Him that He is the most beautiful of the sons of men.

He is the splendor of the eternal glory of the Father.

O God, Who through the Immaculate Conception of the Blessed Virgin prepared a worthy habitation for Your Son, we pray You, that as You preserved her from every stain of sin, in view of the merits of Your Son, to grant to us, too, through her intercession, the grace to come to You with pure hearts.

St. Thomas of Canterbury

St. Thomas of Canterbury had the pious habit of saying seven *Hail Marys* in honor of Mary's seven joys: the Annunciation, the Visitation, the Nativity of Jesus, the Epiphany, the Finding in the Temple, the Resurrection, and the Ascension of Jesus into heaven.

One day the Blessed Virgin appeared to him and said, "Thomas, your devotion is very dear to me, but why do you consider only the joys I experienced on earth? Henceforth, honor also my joys in heaven." Thomas replied, "But how can I know them?" Mary's answer was, "Recite seven *Hail Marys* to commemorate the honor I receive from the Blessed Trinity in paradise; the excellence of virginity; the splendor of the glory rendered by the saints; the praise of the angels; and the increase of extrinsic glory as the fruits of the redemption are applied."

CHAPTER III

THE HAIL MARY—II

And Elizabeth was filled with the Holy Spirit, and cried out with a loud voice, saying: Blessed art thou among women and blessed is the fruit of thy womb! (Luke 1: 41-42).

Holy Mary, Mother of God, pray for us sinners, now and at the hour of our death. Amen.

Following the **praise** is the **petition** to the Madonna. The first part of the Hail Mary exalts the Blessed Virgin, the second exposes our needs. It is a very brief, simple, and humble petition, full of confidence.

The first part of the **Ave** is almost entirely composed of the words of the Holy Spirit; the second, of the words of the Church, guided by the Holy Spirit.

⁂ ⁂ ⁂

1) **Holy Mary.** The word **holy** summarizes the first part of the **Ave**; the name of the Virgin follows next: Mary. Mary's name greatly honors her; it is the most beautiful after that of Jesus. At the sound of Mary's name, heaven exults, hell trembles, and the earth thrills with hope.

By pronouncing Mary's name we place before this exalted queen the interminable chain of gifts she received from God.

The name of Mary rings sweetly in our hearts; it is like a celestial dew which refreshes our spirit.

2) **Mother of God.** This is the great secret of our trust in her.

St. Francis de Sales writes: "If Mary were only Mother of God, I could honor her as sovereign, but I could not hope in her mercy. If Mary were only my Mother, I would confide in her heart, but not in her power. Since, however, Mary is both God's Mother and mine, I have limitless trust in her goodness and power!"

3) **Pray for us sinners.** The Blessed Virgin always answers with favors those who greet her with the Hail Mary. St. Alphonse says: "Whoever greets Mary will also be greeted by her." In fact, St. Bernard once heard a statue of the Blessed Virgin return his greeting, saying, "Hail, Bernard."

"Mary's greeting," says St. Bonaventure, "will be a grace."

4) **Now and at the hour of our death.** Every day, every minute, we need Mary. Time does not lessen our miseries, it rather increases them. As our energies diminish with the years, our battles become more difficult.

The greatest struggle will be that which awaits us at the last hour of life; the devil will then make his supreme attempt.

From this very moment on, let us place ourselves under the protection of her who is to the

Queen of the most holy Rosary, pray for us.

devil, "terrible as an army in battle array;" thus we add, "and at the hour of our death."

Amen is the expression of trust. **Amen** is equivalent to saying: no preoccupation troubles us if Mary is thinking of us. No matter what trials we shall have to face, Mary's protection will assure us of victory. **Amen:** assisted by our Mother, we fear not in life and in death, in time and in eternity.

Let us present ourselves to Mary as sinners, for she has pity on those in misery. Sin is misery so great that it moves Mary to the deepest compassion. She is pleased with our humility just as God was pleased with the prayer of the repentant publican, who, in the rear of the temple, kept striking his breast, saying: "O God, be merciful to me the sinner" (Luke 18: 13).

"With humility and reverence," writes Thomas a Kempis, "with devotion and confidence, I approach you, O Mary, to offer you pleadingly Gabriel's greeting. I offer it to you with my head bowed in an act of reverence and my arms outstretched in a tender sentiment of devoted affection. Moreover, I hope and pray that all the heavenly hosts repeat this same greeting millions and millions of times. I do not know of any homage I could offer you which would be more glorious for you or sweeter for me. Whoever loves you sincerely will heed and believe me; heaven rejoices and earth has good reason to be awed when I say: **Ave Maria.**

"When I say **Ave Maria,** Satan flees and hell trembles. The world no longer attracts me; it rather becomes repugnant to me when I pray: **Ave Maria.**

"When I recite the **Hail Mary,** sadness departs from me and a new joy fills my heart. Coldness vanishes and my heart is enkindled with love when I say, **Ave Maria.** Devotion grows and compunction is born when I say, **Ave Maria.** The soul is delighted and love of good is strengthened when the **Hail Mary** is said: The sweetness of this greeting is so great that neither I nor any other creature can express it. No matter how much may be said of it, immensely greater is that which remains to be said. All I can do is simply fall upon my knees before the Blessed Virgin and repeat, 'Hail **Mary, full of grace....**' This is a prayer of few words, but one filled with great mysteries; it is brief to say, but far reaching in power. It is more precious than gold and sweeter than honey: worthy of being incessantly murmured in one's heart and frequently repeated with one's lips."

The **Our Father** summarizes the prayers addressed to God; the **Hail Mary** summarizes those directed to Mary.

St. Alphonse writes that the Blessed Virgin deeply appreciates this angelic salutation, which renews the joy she first experienced when the Archangel Gabriel announced to her that she was to be the Mother of God.

The Church wants all canonical hours to open and close with the **Our Father** and the **Hail Mary.** And it would be well to begin and conclude with these prayers all our actions, whether spiritual, such as confession, communion, spiritual reading, hearing sermons and the like; or temporal, such as study, working, eating, sleeping.... Happy are those actions which are enclosed between two **Hail Marys.** Happy also are those days that begin and end with the **Ave:** in every temptation, in every danger, in every inclination to anger or joy, always say a **Hail Mary.** St. Grignion De Montfort says that, when the **Hail Mary** is said with attention, devotion, and modesty, it is a hammer against the devil, the sanctification of souls, the joy of angels, the melody of the predestined, the canticle of the New Testament, the delight of Mary and the glory of the Blessed Trinity: "The **Hail Mary** is a heavenly dew which renders the soul fertile; it is a chaste and loving kiss bestowed on Mary; it is a deep red rose presented to her; it is a precious pearl offered to her; it is a chalice of divine nectar lifted to her lips." All these comparisons were also made by Saints.

The history of the **Ave** also records very many miracles. A touching one is connected with the Shrine of Folgoet in Brittany. In the language of that region, Folgoet means, "the crazy man of the forest." Thus was a poor young man called who was filled with great love and devotion for the Madonna. Having become voluntarily a solitary dweller of the forest, he knew only one prayer, the **Hail Mary,** and he recited it unceasingly. After his death a lily blossomed on his grave, and on its petals shone the words, **Ave Maria,** in golden letters. The wonder and holy fervor resulting from this miracle led to the erection of a magnificent shrine.

Grant, we beseech You, O omnipotent God, that Your faithful, who are happy to be under the protection of the Blessed Virgin Mary, may be freed through her intercession from all evils on earth and may merit the reward of eternal joy in heaven.

St. Thomas Aquinas

St. Thomas Aquinas is a great example of devotion to Mary, as also of eminent sanctity and depth of doctrine. While still a child he picked up a bit of paper on which was written the *Hail Mary,* pressed it tightly between his hands, then put it into his mouth and swallowed it. His very first words were: "Ave Maria."

As he grew in years his devotion to Mary became increasingly more affectionate and enlightened. Through Mary, Thomas received the grace of a vocation to the religious life, the strength to withstand all the efforts made to prevent him from realizing it, and the extraordinary wisdom which won for him the glorious title of Angelic Doctor. It is related that his parents strenuously opposed his vocation, even to the point of imprisoning him. They then tempted him in a base fashion, employing a fallen woman. But Thomas invoked Mary's help and, seizing a blazing firebrand from the fireplace, sent the temptress on her way. Thus, he was able to overcome every obstacle and become a religious.

Having conquered this temptation, Thomas merited to be girded with the cincture of purity by the hands of an Angel; in him every movement of concupiscence was stilled. He maintained his virginal purity perfectly until death. In him were verified the words of the Savior: "Blessed are the clean of heart, for they shall see God" (Matt. 5: 8).

CHAPTER IV

THE HAIL HOLY QUEEN—I

Now therefore, ye children, hear me: Blessed are they that keep my ways. Hear instruction and be wise, and refuse it not. Blessed is the man that heareth me, and that watcheth daily at my gates, and waiteth at the posts of my doors. He that shall find me, shall find life, and shall have salvation from the Lord (Prov. 8: 32-35).

The **Hail Holy Queen** repeats many truths of the **Hail Mary,** but it is a more tender expression. Filial confidence in Mary attains its highest peak in this prayer. The thought which pervades the entire **Hail Holy Queen** is that Mary was made Queen so that she might place all her power at our service.

A single loving glance of hers is enough to give us relief from our ills, to help us overcome all temptation, and to lead us to the vision of Jesus. The **Hail Holy Queen** expresses this truth so clearly, so movingly, and with such psychological penetration that it is truly a practical and theological masterpiece. St. Alphonse was so enthusiastic about this prayer that he explained it at length and devoted to it the principal part of his great work, "The Glories of Mary." "In this book," says the Saint, "leaving other authors to describe the other prerogatives of Mary, I confine myself for the most part to that of her mercy and powerful intercession; having collected, as far as I was able, and with the labor of many years, all that the holy Fathers and most celebrated writers have said of the mercy and power of Mary.

*   *   *

Hail is an expression of joy, a wish and a greeting. The soul rejoices with Mary because she is great by nature and by grace.

The soul wishes that heaven and earth may recognize Mary as Queen: that her mercy may populate heaven with saints.

I want to say **hail** to Mary: celestial vision of love, hope, and beauty; I want to say it with deep reverence as did the Archangel Gabriel, when he presented himself to her as ambassador of God and messenger of the Incarnation: "Hail, full of grace" (Luke 1: 28).

I want to say to Mary, **hail,** with the dispositions of St. Joseph when he recognized her as the virgin spouse destined for him by God—the virgin spouse, whose purity he was to guard; the virgin spouse, with whom he shared sorrows and joys, merit and glory.

I want to say **hail** with the dispositions of St. Elizabeth when she said: "And how have I deserved that the Mother of my Lord should come to me? For behold, the moment that the sound of thy

Immaculate Queen of Peace, pray for us.

greeting came to my ears, the babe in my womb
leapt for joy. And blessed is she who has believed,
because the things promised her by the Lord shall
be accomplished" (Luke 1: 43-45).

I want to say **hail** as do the angels in heaven
when they draw near to this Queen to pay homage
to her, to receive her orders, and to join with her in
the song of the Magnificat.

I want to say **hail** with the dispositions of the
Child Jesus when His glance met His Mother's with
ineffable love, as she approached His little bed in
the morning.

Holy Queen—The Blessed Virgin is called
Queen of Apostles, Queen of Prophets, Queen of
Patriarchs, Queen of Martyrs, and Queen of all
Saints. In fact, in her are gathered all the virtues,
graces, and glories, which are found distributed a-
mong the blessed inhabitants of heaven; moreover,
in her they are of an immensely superior degree. In
Mary there are also many privileges, graces, and
distinctions that were not granted to any other saint.
Finally, through Mary everything that is beautiful
and great passed to the saints. Mary was born
Queen because she was destined to be the Mother
of the supreme King, Jesus; she was crowned Queen
when she entered heaven and was exalted above all
creatures. The Liturgy says of her: "The Holy
Mother of God has been exalted above the choirs

of angels in the celestial kingdoms"; she is the daughter of God and the spouse of the Holy Spirit, and also by reason of these privileges she is Queen.

Mary is Queen of heaven and earth; she is Queen of purgatory, of the missions, of the rosary, of peace—the universal Queen.

St. Bernardine of Siena writes: "As many creatures as there are who serve God, so many they are who serve Mary; for as angels and men, and all things that are in heaven and on earth, are subject to the empire of God, so are they also under the dominion of Mary."

My Queen, I, too, wish to be one of your loving subjects; with the spirit of St. Grignion De Montfort, I declare myself a servant and slave of your love today and always. I am certain that if I am your affectionate subject on earth, I shall also be a co-citizen of that heavenly Jerusalem, where, together with your Son, you reign forever and ever.

Mother—Mary is our Mother. She loves us with a love that surpasses that of all mothers and this for various reasons: love of God and love of neighbor are in proportion to each other, for they are two flames of the same fire. St. Paul, in fact, was tireless in his zeal for men because his love for Jesus Christ was limitless. The Madonna loved the Lord more than anyone else; for this reason she loves us more than do all the angels and saints.

Mary loves us because from the cross Jesus Christ entrusted us to her maternal care; for her, every recommendation made by Jesus is sacred.

Mary loves us because we are poor, miserable, and ill; a mother is overwhelmed with anguish at the bedside of her son. Thus, Mary is called a free public hospital. Two qualifications are necessary for entrance: evidence of poverty and illness, the most destitute and most critically ill always being preferred.

In pain Mary brought us forth to a life of grace. That which costs the most is most dear. We truly cost Mary many sorrows, especially on Calvary. There Mary became Queen of Martyrs for us.

Of Mercy—Ministry of justice was not assigned to the Blessed Virgin; it was rather reserved for her Son. To Mary was entrusted the distribution of grace.

This charge of hers is special: 1) because through her intercession, sinners, who wish to do so, can escape divine justice while they are yet on earth by taking refuge in her, beseeching grace for a true repentance, a holy confession, and stable amendment of their lives. 2) because of that which St. Bernard says to Mary: "You are the Queen of Mercy, and I am the most miserable sinner of all. Thus, if I am the most wretched of your subjects, you must take more care of me than of all the others. Could you perhaps reject the cause of the most miserable when you have been designated Queen for the miserable?" 3) Mary is especially the Mother of sinners who want to amend their lives. She has the same inclinations as the Heart of Jesus, Who came to save that which was lost; united to the very mission of her Son, she wishes to seek the lost sheep and the missing drachma. **I am the Mother of sinners who want to amend their ways.** It is the sick who need a doctor.

Our Life—Mary is the life of the soul that lives of Jesus, of grace, and of supernatural spirit.

We seek for grace and we seek it by Mary.

St. Alphonse prayed thus to the Madonna: "O my Mother, Mary, I have great confidence in you. It is from you that I await the grace to repent my sins and the fortitude to keep from falling again. If I am ill, you are my doctor. I know that your heart finds comfort in helping the afflicted. Therefore, console me, console your heart, and console the Heart of Jesus: I beg you for the grace of God."

Our Sweetness—Living with our heavenly Mother is a great comfort in every hour of our lives. Mary lifts us up and even carries us, if necessary. Voluntary orphans are foolish: even Jesus wanted this Mother and shall we be so rash as to refuse her?

Let us beg Mary for consolation. St. Bernard exhorted thus: "O man, whoever you are, understand that in this world you are tossed about on a stormy and tempestuous sea, rather than walking on solid ground; remember that if you would avoid being drowned, you must never turn your eyes from this star, Mary. Keep them fixed on the star; invoke Mary. In dangers of sinning, when molested by temptations, when doubtful as to how you should act, remember that Mary can help you, and that, when you call upon her, she will instantly succor you. Your heart should never lose confidence in her holy name, nor should your lips ever cease to invoke it.

"If you follow Mary, you will not go astray of the paths of salvation. If she supports you, you cannot fall. If she protects you, you have nothing to fear, for you cannot be lost. If she guides you, you will not be weary, for your salvation will be worked out with ease. In short, if Mary undertakes your defense, you are certain of gaining the kingdom of heaven."

Mary is sweetness for the dying. When at the point of death, St. John of God awaited Mary's visit, and because she delayed coming, he was afflicted. But when it was time, the divine Mother appeared and reproved him, saying, "My John, what were you thinking? That I had abandoned you? And do you not know that at the hour of death I know not how to abandon my devotees? See, I have come to take you; let us go to heaven." Shortly afterwards, the saint expired.

Our Hope—We hope that Mary, through her intercession, will obtain for us heaven and the graces necessary to attain it.

St. Bonaventure's sentiments are tender: "If my Redeemer rejects me on account of my sins, I will cast myself at the feet of His Mother, Mary, and there I will remain prostrate until she has obtained my forgiveness. For this Mother of Mercy knows not how to do otherwise than compassionate the miserable who fly to her for help. If not out of duty, at least out of compassion she will engage her Son to pardon me."

"Look down upon us, then, O most compassionate Mother," let us conclude in the words of Euthymius; "look down upon us, for we are your servants and in you we have placed all our confidence."

Mary's beneficial assistance is continual, accompanying us from birth until death.

Lord Jesus Christ, Who willed that Mary, Your Mother, might be also our Mother so as to help us at every instant, grant, we beseech Thee, that by diligently imploring her maternal help, we may always experience the fruits of Your redemption.

St. Vincent de Paul and the Hail Holy Queen

One day when St. Vincent de Paul was going from Marseilles to Toulouse, he was taken prisoner by some Turkish pirates. As was their custom, they led their captive to a public square to be sold. After passing through the hands of two or three Mohammedans, he fell into the power of an apostate Christian from Nice, who was waiting at the market in Tunis.

This master was worse than the pirates and very fierce. Vincent's patience, however, made a great impression on his master and on his master's wife.

One day the latter said to Vincent,

"Vincent, sing us a beautiful song about your religion."

"Ah, my lady," answered Vincent, "whoever is far from his native land cannot sing songs of joy. How can we sing in a foreign land? In my religion there is, however, one canticle that suits me as a poor exile and I want to sing it for you." So saying, he intoned the Hail Holy Queen with such sweetness and sadness that he moved his owners to tears. From that day on, they were won by the saint's virtues and shortly after, were converted.

Thus, with the Blessed Virgin's help, the saint of charity freed himself from corporal chains and returned to his owners their holy liberty as children of God.

CHAPTER V

THE HAIL HOLY QUEEN—II

I cried to Thee, O Lord: I said: Thou art my hope, my portion in the land of the living (Ps. 141: 6).

To thee do we cry, poor banished children of Eve.

We are Eve's children by birth, but we are also Mary's children by redemption: to thee do we cry, poor, banished children of Eve, to become, O Mary, your children in the spirit, as Jesus wills; whereas, according to the flesh, we are children of Eve. Eve is the woman conquered by the devil; Mary is the conqueror of the devil.

As Eve's children we are born in sin; as Mary's children we are reborn through grace.

Eve is a perfect example of the imprudent, weak woman; Mary, the perfect example of the prudent, strong woman.

As Eve's childen we are subject to three concupiscences: avarice, pride and lust. As Mary's children we seek humility, poverty and purity.

Three truths make us hope in Mary: she knows our needs; she has compassion on us and wants to help us; she has riches for us all.

Mary knows our needs. Many are our spiritual and material necessities. With regard to our body we need food, clothing, health, shelter and the means to do good. With regard to our spirit, we must conquer sin, triumph over the devil's temptations, dominate our passions and detach ourselves from the world; we need grace, living faith, strong hope and love of God. We must fulfill the mission which God has entrusted to each of us, remain firm in life's many trials, die a holy death and gain heaven.

Moreover, from Eve's sin have stemmed so many serious evils that no one will ever be able to describe them fully. They are the painful trials of life, which are so frequent that we often grow weary of carrying our cross: physical sufferings, of every kind, moral suffering, sadness, doubts, ignorance, deceptions, the ill will of enemies and treachery of friends.

For a son, however, it is always a great comfort to open his heart to his mother. So, too, for us, children of Mary, it is sweet consolation to bare our souls in front of an image of Mary.

Mary knows our needs because she, too, is Eve's daughter. And if through God's singular mercy, she was exempt from the evils that are consequences of sin, she was not exempt from suffering. In fact, she is the woman who suffered more than all others, so much that she became the Queen of martyrs.

Mother of orphans, pray for us.

The Madonna shed many tears: "And thy own soul a sword shall pierce" (Luke 2: 35), said the elderly Simeon. The life of Jesus was sought from His infancy and the world's hatred was not even appeased when it saw Him crucified and buried. Mary saw Him Who is the most beautiful of men, because He is the true Son of God, reduced to a state comparable to that of a crushed worm. She heard the blasphemies, she witnessed Judas' betrayal, the persecution of the growing Church, the idolatrous cults, the errors and vices of men. Yes, Mary saw it all.

The Madonna sees our needs in God. She enjoys the beatific vision: in God, as in a perfectly clear mirror, are reflected all our needs; she sees them better than we do.

Mary hears our prayers and our sighs; she heeds our petitions; she is not deaf. More than any other creature, Mary pays attention to us; she understands everyone's language and she comprehends more than human words can express.

At the marriage feast at Cana, Mary proved how quick she is to consider our needs. The first to notice the lack of wine were not the newlyweds or the hosts; it was Mary, instead, who first noticed and provided.

Mary has compassion on us. It is not enough that someone know our needs; that someone must also be moved to compassion at our ills and be able to cure them.

Mary's heart is merciful:

a) Because it is the heart most like the Heart of Jesus. From Mary's blood was formed the Heart of the adorable Lamb Who redeemed the world.

Jesus was most sensitive to all the sufferings of humanity: "I have compassion on the crowd" (Mark 8: 2); in a similar manner, Mary's knowledge of our infirmities is not sterile; in her, seeing suffering and being moved to compassion are one and the same thing.

b) Because Mary is our Mother. When a person is elected to an office, he is endowed with all the gifts and qualities necessary to fulfill his duties. Now, our concept of a mother differs from our concept of a father: in a mother, heart, compassion and loving anxiety rule; in a father, strength, intelligence and work.

c) Man's experience proves this. St. Bernard summarizes the story of Mary's mercies in these words: "Mary became all to all; to all she offers the bosom of her mercy, that all may receive of it: the slave, his redemption; the infirm, health; the afflicted, comfort; the sinner, pardon; and God, glory— that there should be no one who would not feel her warmth and great affection."

In the twelfth century, the greater part of Spain suffered under the cruel yoke of Saracen oppression.

St. Peter Nolasco, when still a young man, went from France to Spain and gave away his great wealth to ransom Christians enslaved by the Turks. He even expressed the desire to be sold himself to replace the poor slaves.

One night, while he was considering this idea, the Madonna appeared to him, her face most serene. She told him that she and her Son would be most pleased if an Order were founded with the special mission of freeing Christians enslaved by the Turks.

St. Peter went to his confessor, Raymond of Penafort. On that very night the Blessed Virgin had also appeared to St. Raymond and expressed the same desire to him. While the two men of God were conferring, James, the King of Aragon, arrived. The Madonna had also appeared to him that night and had told him to help the Order that she wished founded in her honor.

On August 10, 1218, the three men started the new religious Order and named it after Our Lady.

Mary is able to help us. Mary has riches for all. Mary has power for every weakness. Mary is a refuge for all who are lost.

The reasons are many:

1. Mary is as powerful with God as she was holy on earth. Whoever practiced on earth a virtue has the power in heaven of obtaining that virtue for others. Whoever practiced several virtues has the

power of obtaining those same virtues. Mary practiced them all; therefore, she has power to obtain them all. Thus she is invoked for purity as well as for strength; for zeal as well as for wisdom; in times of heresy as in calamities, such as war or plagues; in struggles of the spirit against the flesh as in sicknesses of the body and temporal dangers.

2. All that is divided in the saints is united in Mary. We invoke St. Louis for purity, St. Thomas Aquinas for knowledge, St. Francis de Sales for meekness; we beg the Apostles for zeal, the martyrs for patience, and the confessors for faith; we pray to St. Lucy for eyesight, St. Camillus of Lellis for the dying, St. Vincent de Paul for charitable works; St. John Vianney as protector of parishes and St. Jerome Emiliani as protector of orphans.

3. Moreover, as Mother of God, Mary has power surpassing that of all the saints.

Great is the authority of mothers over their sons, as great was Mary's authority over Jesus; and even should the sons be monarchs, mothers never become their subjects. It is true that Jesus now sits at the right hand of the Father in heaven; that is, as St. Thomas explains, even as man, He has supreme dominion over all creatures, including the Blessed Virgin; nevertheless, at one time, on this earth, He willed to be subject to Mary: "And He was subject to them" (Luke 2: 51).

Virgins follow the divine Lamb wherever He leads them: "These follow the Lamb wherever he goes" (Apoc. 14: 4). The Lamb, on the contrary, followed Mary on this earth, having become subject to her.

Even though Mary can no longer command her Son in heaven, her prayers are always those of a mother and, therefore, most powerful. St. Bonaventure says that Mary's great privilege is that, with her Son, she is most powerful to obtain whatever she wills.

Mary was crowned Queen by the Blessed Trinity. St. Bernardine of Siena declares that all obey Mary's commands, even God; by this he means to say that God grants her prayers as if they were commands.

The Mother has the same power as the Son. Mary was made omnipotent by Jesus Who is omnipotent: the Son is omnipotent by nature, the Mother by grace.

Jesus is somewhat of a debtor to Mary. Thus, almost as if to fulfill His obligation to this Mother for giving Him human nature through her consent, He grants all her requests.

Therefore, let us take refuge in Mary; she is a powerful, merciful, and understanding Mother.

O God, Who, to free faithful Christians from the power of pagans, deigned by means of Your Son's most glorious

Mother to enrich Your Church with a new family, grant
that as we piously venerate her as institutor of this family,
we may be equally freed, through her merits and her inter-
cession, from all sin and the slavery of the devil.

St. Francis Xavier

The great Apostle of India and Japan, Francis Xavier,
honored the Mother of God throughout his life with the
most intimate devotion and strong love. It was in Paris, on
the feast of the Presentation, in the Church of Montmartre
dedicated to the Blessed Virgin, that Francis Xavier, together with St. Ignatius and his companions, consecrated
himself to God with the holy vows.

It was in the Church at Loretto, later, that he was first
inspired to go to India to preach the Gospel.

Francis Xavier sought God's grace only through Mary's
intercession and never undertook any work without first
entrusting it to Mary's patronage.

CHAPTER VI

THE HAIL HOLY QUEEN—III

Upon the rivers of Babylon, there we sat and wept: when we remembered Sion: on the willows in the midst thereof we hung up our instruments. For there they that led us into captivity required of us the words of songs.

Sing ye to us a hymn of the songs of Sion.

How shall we sing the song of the Lord in a strange land? (Ps. 136, 1-4.)

To Mary do we send up our sighs, mourning and weeping in this valley of tears.

Two things have made devotion to Mary both spontaneous and universal: our innumerable needs on the one hand and the Madonna's motherly goodness on the other.

Mary, Mother of the Church — The Church is a supernatural society, instituted by Jesus Christ to instruct, guide and sanctify men. She is the mystical body of Jesus Christ. The Church is carried in the arms of Mary, as Jesus Christ also was carried in her arms.

At the annunciation, Mary consented to be the Mother of Jesus Christ and she devoted herself completely to her mission, fulfilling it perfectly.

At the foot of the cross, Mary accepted the care of the Church and daily she carries out this duty.

Pope Pius XI says: "Whoever studies the annals of the Catholic Church diligently will easily discover, bound up with every record of Christianity, the powerful patronage of the Virgin Mother of God. In public misfortune as well as in private need, the faithful of every epoch beseechingly turned to Mary that, in her goodness, she might succor them, obtaining for them from God help and relief in their needs of soul and body. And her most powerful help was never awaited in vain by those who implored her with devout, trusting prayers."

A splendid example is the victory of the Christians over the Turks at Lepanto, a victory attributed to the holy Rosary.

❊   ❊   ❊

Mary is powerful against heresy. Heresy is obstinacy in error regarding matters of faith. Mary is a hammer against heresy itself, but she is salvation for separated brethren of good will.

Down through the centuries, the Blessed Virgin has defended the Church against heresy. She has converted heretics and reconciled schismatics.

In a special manner, Mary assisted St. John the Evangelist, who wrote his gospel against the first heretics.

Nestorius denied the divinity of Jesus Christ and the divine maternity of Mary. The Madonna, however, raised up St. Cyril of Alexandria to the defense of truth, and the Fathers of the Council of Ephesus proclaimed the true faith. Then was sung the antiphon: "Hail, O perpetual Virgin, you alone have destroyed all the heresies of the world."

The Albigensians were conquered and converted in large numbers by St. Dominic with the holy Rosary.

In the nineteenth century it was the Immaculate Conception who, through the work of Pius XI and her apparitions at Lourdes, destroyed rationalism and naturalism.

And if Leo XIII was called the Pope of the Rosary, his successor, Pius X, was the hammer against modernism.

Thus Pius XI wrote: "When widespread error was bent upon rending the seamless garment of the Church and throwing the Catholic world into confusion, our fathers turned trustingly to her who alone destroyed all the heresies of the world, and the victory won by her brought the return of better times."

Mary, seat of wisdom — In Mary dwelt eternal Wisdom descended from heaven to teach men. For this reason Mary is patroness of studies. From her St. John Damascene received his wisdom; from her St. Albert the Great received the grace to progress in his studies to the extent that he was able to teach

O Queen, you are the beauty of Carmel,
pray for us.

in every field of knowledge; from her St. Thomas Aquinas sought celestial wisdom daily with the holy Rosary.

Mary taught the Apostles the mysteries of the Incarnation, infancy, and private life of Jesus.

Mary is invoked by the great band of missionary societies: Dominicans, Franciscans, Carmelites, Jesuits, Servites, Salesians, etc. From Mary, the Doctors of the Church and Catholic writers have always sought and received enlightenment. From Mary, the Pontiffs have sought and obtained wisdom and counsel to govern the Christian people.

Mary and temporal needs — Nations at war have always taken refuge in Mary and wonderful Christian victories have given proof of her power: Lepanto, Vienna, Murret, Temesvar and Corfu are notable events.

Mary well deserves the title conferred upon her by Benedict XV: **Queen of Peace.**

The sick in great numbers have taken refuge in Mary. At Lourdes, trainloads of sick people arrive from every part of the world. Some of these sick are critically ill and their cases have been declared hopeless by medical science. There it can be said that the blind see, the deaf hear, the lame walk, the tubercular and those afflicted with every infirmity are cured.

Mary and moral needs — In the lives of the saints we often read of vexing temptations being converted to splendid victories through Mary's intercession. So it was with St. Benedict, St. Bernard, St. Niles, St. Alphonse Rodriguez and thousands of others.

Our faith is strengthened when we read in the lives of Cajetan of Thiene, Francis Regis, Clare of Assisi and innumerable others that they were provided miraculously with money and provisions by the Blessed Virgin. We find that she comforts those who are calumniated, oppressed or persecuted; she is solace in sadness, depression or anguish.

How right St. Lawrence Justinian was to call Mary: "Sweet comfort of our pilgrimage." And since sinners are the most miserable of all men, Mary continuously prays to her Son for them.

O God, Who through the Blessed Virgin's Immaculate Conception prepared a worthy habitation for Your Son, we humbly beg You that, by commemorating Mary's apparition, we may attain salvation of soul and body.

St. Elizabeth, Virgin

Elizabeth was afflicted by both interior suffering and corporal infirmities. One day, being privileged to see Mary Most Holy surrounded by chaste and holy virgins, she prayed thus: "O holy Virgin, have pity on me! What cruel tribulations oppress me! Have compassion on me, for sorrows have tormented me from childhood, and at present my life is a continuous martyrdom!"

Mary answered her sweetly, "My daughter, the Lord tries you in this life, but He will console you in the next;

He wants to purify you on this earth so that after death you may enjoy rest and eternal happiness. See these virgins who surround me: they suffered for love of God, and now they are not only honored in His eyes, but before all men."

Filled with new strength by these words, Elizabeth maintained great serenity of soul in the midst of all her tribulations, from then on. Her sole consolation in her last hour was to invoke the name of Mary, and in Mary's arms she piously expired.

CHAPTER VII

THE HAIL HOLY QUEEN—IV

Behold, He comes with the clouds, and every eye shall see Him, and they also who pierced Him. And all the tribes of the earth shall wail over Him (Apoc. 1: 7).

Turn then, most gracious advocate, thine eyes of mercy toward us.

All graces are transfused from the head, Jesus Christ, to His mystical body by means of Mary.

"Mary," says St. Alphonse, "is all eyes to discover our infirmities and help us." The first misery from which she wishes to free us, however, is sin. If God bears an infinite hatred for sin, Mary hates sin with an immense hatred.

Mary hates sin because it offends the Lord, infinite majesty; sin is supreme ingratitude to God's goodness; sin renews the passion of Jesus Christ.

Sin is both the spiritual and material ruination of Mary's children. The Holy Spirit says: "A curse, if you obey not the commandments of the Lord your God" (Deut. 11: 28).

Mary came into the world to make reparation for sin by giving us Jesus, about Whom John the Baptist said: "Behold, the Lamb of God, Who takes away the sin of the world!" (John 1: 29). It had been predicted: "that sin may have an end, and iniquity may be abolished" (Dan. 9: 24).

The just on this earth are not exempt from the devil's temptations; they are as much subject to them as sinners and perhaps even more so.

As a good mother, Mary spurs us on to virtue—now, with inspirations; at another time, with special graces; and again, with consolations. She encouraged St. Margaret Mary Alacoque to bear persecutions patiently; she ordered St. Louis and St. Stanislaus Kostka to become religious in the Society of Jesus; she taught the way of perfection to St. Mary Magdalen dei Pazzi and St. Rose of Lima.

Mary strengthens the just to persevere. She begs God to obtain perseverance for the just; she prompts them to ask for it incessantly.

Before beginning His passion, our Divine Redeemer ardently begged the Eternal Father to grant perseverance to His disciples: Holy Father, watch over this group, that no one may fail. Mary, who has the spirit of Jesus, does the very same.

For those who have fallen into sin Mary performs two tasks: she defends them before divine justice and invites them to conversion. St. Alphonse says: "If you fear to have recourse to Jesus Christ, because His justice frightens you, and you wish another advocate with this mediator, go to Mary. She will intercede for you with her Son." St. Bernard says: "This divine Mother is the ladder of sinners; she is my greatest confidence, she is the whole ground of my hope."

Sweet Heart of Mary, be my salvation.

Mary invites sinners to conversion. She studies the most efficacious ways and most opportune moments. She spurs them on with bitter remorse, which torments them day and night, thus giving them the urge to seek God. How many there are who with tears in their eyes have declared that they know it was this good Mother who led them to God!

She welcomes them as soon as they return. Jesus has never driven away anyone; in fact, He said that He came to save sinners: "For the Son of Man came to seek and to save what was lost" (Luke 19: 10). Like Jesus, Mary has always welcomed sinners lovingly; she has said that she is their Mother.

St. Ephrem calls her: refuge of sinners; St. Bernard: ladder of sinners; St. Lawrence Justinian: hope of the erring; St. Thomas of Villanova: the shortest and easiest way to reach God.

Mary's greatest glory, however, is in the changing of sinners to saints. She not only puts them back on the right path, but, if they do not resist, she strives to transform them into vessels of election and to make them saints.

She granted great favors to Margaret of Cortona, who was a sinner; to Mary of Egypt, famous for her dissolute life; to William of Aquitania, noted for his cruelty: Mary made them saints.

For all sinners Mary is ever a powerful, universal and merciful advocate. "Be comforted then, O you who fear," says St. Thomas of Villanova;

"breathe freely and take courage, O wretched sinners; this great Virgin who is Mother of your Judge, is also the advocate of the whole human race; fit for this office, for she can do what she wills with God; most wise, for she knows all the means of appeasing Him; universal, for she welcomes all, and refuses to defend no one."

O God, Whose only begotten Son purchased for us the rewards of eternal life, grant, we beseech Thee, that, meditating upon the mysteries in the Most Holy Rosary of the Blessed Virgin, we may imitate what they contain and obtain what they promise.

The Victory of Pelagio

Christian people have never had recourse to Mary in vain. Spain experienced her help when suffering under Moorish oppression. One outstanding event occurred in 718. King Pelagio and one thousand men had entrenched themselves in a cavern deemed inaccessible. Alamona, with eighty thousand Moors, violently assaulted the grotto, while Pelagio and his men called upon Mary's help. Rocks and arrows bombarded the assailants until they were constrained to flee in haste. Pelagio pursued them and twenty thousand Moors were killed on the battlefield with their general. The others drowned in the Reva River.

A similar prodigy occurred in 1583, on the feast of the Purification of the Blessed Virgin, when three hundred Portuguese and thirty thousand Ethiopians defeated the army of the King of Angola, an army of one million, two hundred thousand soldiers. Nearly all of the latter perished—either by arrows or by falling into a great abyss.

CHAPTER VIII

THE HAIL HOLY QUEEN—V

For Thou, my God, hast heard my prayer: Thou hast given an inheritance to them that fear Thy name.

So will I sing a psalm to Thy name for ever and ever: that I may pay my vows from day to day (Ps. 60: 6-9).

And after this our exile show unto us the blessed fruit of thy womb, Jesus. St. Bernard says: "Mary is a full aqueduct, that others may receive of her plenitude. Before the birth of the Blessed Virgin, a constant flow of graces was wanting, because this aqueduct did not exist. But now that Mary has been given to the world, heavenly graces constantly flow through her on all."

Let us consider:

1. Devotion to Mary is morally necessary; 2. Mary frees us from purgatory; 3. A devotee of Mary is saved.

1) **Necessity of devotion to Mary.** The principal grace that we intend to obtain with certainty through Mary is heaven.

The intercession of saints is most helpful; devotion to the Blessed Virgin is morally necessary for our eternal salvation. Jesus Christ is Mediator by right; Mary is mediatrix by grace.

According to St. Anselm, devotion to Mary is necessary so that the dignity of the mediator may make up for our own lack.

To pray to Mary is not to distrust divine mercy, but it is to fear our own unworthiness. This doctrine is taught by St. Augustine, St. Alphonse, St. Germanus, St. Anselm, St. John Damascene, St. Bonaventure, St. Anthony, St. Bernardine of Siena, and all Catholic theologians.

St. Alphonse writes: "Whoever believes not in this teaching shows little devotion for Mary; I would not like to be numbered among them, nor would I like my reader to be one of them."

Devotion to Mary is of moral necessity on account of the extreme difficulties in which we live: man resembles a battered ship; the sea—that is, the world—is most dangerous, for many are the treacheries of enemy ships.

St. Anselm writes: "It is impossible that a devotee of Mary who faithfully pays homage to her and recommends his soul to her be damned. This applies to true devotees, who wish to amend their lives, not to those who make abuse of this devotion to sin more.

2) **Efficacy of the devotion to Mary.** Devotion to Mary is a means of avoiding or shortening one's purgatory.

St. Alphonse says: "The poor souls in purgatory are helped by Mary much more than are the souls still living on earth. In fact, these souls are more worthy of mercy since they are unable to help themselves."

St. Bernardine of Siena says: "In that prison, where souls espoused to Jesus Christ are detained, Mary has a certain dominion and plenitude of power, not only to relieve them, but even to deliver them from their pains."

The Church has approved the Religious Institute of "Our Lady of Suffrage" which has the purpose of praying to Mary for the souls in purgatory. The Sisters of this Institute call Mary, Queen of Purgatory and Mother of those holy souls.

The Blessed Virgin helps all the souls in purgatory, but the first to receive help and relief are her devotees. "See of what consequence it is to be the servant of this good Lady, for she never forgets her servants when they are suffering in those flames; for though Mary relieves all suffering souls in purgatory, yet she always obtains far greater indulgence and relief for her own clients" (Novarinus).

The promise made by Mary to Pope John XXII is a singular privilege. While he was praying, she appeared to him, clothed in dazzling light and holding the scapular of Carmel in her hands. Among other things, she said: "If religious or lay members of Carmel go to purgatory for their sins, as a loving Mother I will descend in their midst on the Saturday following their death and I will lead them to the

O heart most pure of the Blessed Virgin Mary,
obtain for me from Jesus a pure and humble heart.

holy mountain of eternal life." Thus the pontiff records the words of Mary in the famous bull of March 3, 1332, commonly called the Sabbatine Bull.

Because of Mary's maternal compassion, the Church entrusts to her the cause of the suffering souls in purgatory, that through the intercession of the Blessed Virgin and all the Saints, God may deign to call them to the enjoyment of eternal happiness.

3) **How and when to practice devotion to Mary.** Here let us consider that whoever is greatly devoted to Mary becomes a saint. This method is explained as follows by St. Methodius, who says to Mary, **"You, O great Mother, are the beginning, the middle and the end of our happiness."**

a) Mary is the **beginning**, because she helps us find grace. A sinner who has recourse to Mary will be converted. The lives of Mary of Egypt, Alphonse Ratisbonne, Margaret of Cortona, and many others give proof of this truth.

Furthermore, we have the daily experience of the conversions of heretics, pagans, apostates, schismatics, unbelievers, blasphemers, Communists, etc.

b) Mary is the **middle** of our salvation. In fact, through Mary, the innocent preserve their baptismal candor, and the penitent persevere on the right path.

When St. Bernardine of Siena was a child he was in very grave danger. When Bernardine was three he lost his mother; at the age of six he lost his father and was taken in by his cousin, Tobia, who guarded his virtue jealously. At the age of eleven he was taken to Siena.

One day Bernardine said to his cousin, "Do you know that I am so much in love with a beautiful lady that I would willingly give my life to enjoy her presence, and if I were to spend a day without seeing her I would not be able to sleep at night?"

Tobia was amazed and decided secretly to keep a watchful eye on her young cousin.

One day Bernardine went to the Camollian gate, where a beautiful picture of the Madonna of the Angels was venerated. He knelt in meditation, prayed devoutly, and then returned home. His cousin followed him there for several days. Finally she asked the boy to tell her everything.

The innocent and chaste Bernardine hid nothing: "My cousin, since you wish it, I shall tell you my secret. I am inflamed with love for the Blessed Virgin Mary, Mother of God." And throughout his life, Bernardine persevered in his devotion to the Madonna of the Angels, who today is venerated in the Church of St. Luke in Siena.

Mary protected Bernardine's baptismal innocence and the lily of his virginity from the thorns of life's temptations. He, in turn, abandoned profane studies, received and followed the vocation to the religious life and to the apostolate.

c) Mary is the **end** of sanctification. While a student in Paris, St. Francis de Sales consecrated his purity to the Blessed Virgin in the Church of St. Stephen.

He was called to be an affable spiritual director who facilitates the way of perfection: the great doctor of devotion and piety. A painful trial awaited him, however. Francis, who loved the Lord so greatly, became insensible and arid in his spiritual life; he was oppressed by a terrifying fear that he was not in the grace of God. The temptation lasted for six weeks. During this trial, the young man became so sick with grief that his faithful servant thought he was lost.

One day Francis entered St. Stephen's Church and in the abyss of his misery, went straight to the Madonna's altar and burst into tears. He recited St. Bernard's sweet prayer: "Remember, O most gracious Virgin Mary," and he added: "O God, if it is decreed that I should not love You in Heaven, at least allow me to love You on earth with all my strength." Our Lady came to his aid. His nightmare ended, and, thus, Francis regained both health and joy: to the grace of liberation from the temptation followed the grace of the religious vocation.

Francis wrote the "Introduction to a Devout Life" and "The Love of God" and dedicated them to Mary. They are learned works, in which a method of spiritual life is explained.

Every year, on the feast of the Purification, Francis renewed his vow of chastity, and every day, in fulfillment of a vow, he recited the entire Rosary.

Lord Jesus Christ, since You wished that the Blessed Virgin Mary, Your Immaculate Mother, from her conception, be resplendent for her innumerable gifts, grant, that by continually imploring her patronage, we may attain to eternal joys.

A Deathbed Conversion

In 1856, in Paris, an unknown person earnestly sought a priest to bring the comforts of the Faith to a dying man.

Upon entering the designated apartment, the priest found a young girl, who was struggling to control her emotion. Sobbing, she told the priest that her dying father had absolutely no belief in religion and that he had ordered his family to let him die in peace. She feared that the sight of a priest would cause him to become furious and die suddenly.

The priest consoled the afflicted girl, advised her to entrust herself to Mary's patronage, and urged her to recite the Rosary softly at her father's bedside so as to arouse in him religious sentiments.

At nightfall the sick man called his daughter and said, "You won't leave me alone tonight, will you?"

At her father's bedside the young girl, with tears in her eyes, recited the Rosary softly. The dying man was suffering more in soul than in body; he watched his daughter with obvious tenderness. The girl's serenity deeply contrasted with her father's agitation.

When the Rosary was completed, the suffering man drew a deep sigh:

"Oh, if I only had faith!"

At this sudden revelation, the daughter said tearfully, "I have prayed to the Blessed Virgin to give you this heavenly gift; you pray to her also, dear father."

That night the sick man dreamed that he was struggling in a roaring current and was unable to reach the other bank, where his beloved daughter awaited him, arms wide open to receive him. Suddenly a woman of marvelous beauty took him affectionately by the hand and showed him an enormous bridge with one hundred fifty arches, which led safely to the other shore. Upon awakening he related his dream to his daughter, who explained it to him. The woman was the Blessed Virgin; the bridge with the one hundred fifty arches was the Rosary, by means of which he should gain heaven. The poor old man wept with deep emotion and requested a priest that he might make his confession and receive Communion. He died an edifying death.

CHAPTER IX

THE HAIL HOLY QUEEN—VI

I am the Mother of fair love, and of fear, and of knowledge, and of holy hope. In me is all grace of the way and of the truth, in me is all hope of life and of virtue (Ecclus. 24: 24-25).

O clement, O loving, O sweet Virgin Mary.

St. Bernard has a beautiful interpretation of this phrase: Mary is clement with **penitents,** freeing them from their sins; she is compassionate to **those who wish to advance in virtue;** she is sweet to those who love her, that is, to the **perfect.**

"Mary is clement with the miserable, compassionate towards those who pray to her, sweet towards those who love her. She shows herself clement in delivering us from chastisement, compassionate in bestowing graces, and sweet in giving herself to those who seek her."

❄ ❄ ❄

Mary is clement with penitents. After helping sinners to repent and to obtain pardon, Mary obtains for them the grace of **perseverance.**

After confession, the devil comes back to the attack. It is one thing to detest sin, but it is quite another matter to conquer bad habits, flee from occasions of sin, and subdue passions.

Perseverance is the virtue that assures the soul of paradise, but it requires many victories. St. Augustine speaks of the devil's attacks after his conversion. Many times, St. Pelagia was tempted to return to her former scandalous way of living. Margaret of Cortona and St. Mary of Egypt often were likewise tempted, but the Blessed Virgin obtained perseverance for them.

According to the council of Trent, perseverance is a free gift, which cannot be merited by us. However, it will be obtained, affirm St. Augustine and Suarez, by those who faithfuly ask for it.

St. Anselm makes a statement which at first causes wonder: "We often more quickly obtain what we ask by calling on the name of Mary than by invoking that of Jesus." Is it not true that God's goodness is infinite, whereas Mary's is finite? This is indeed true, but the Blessed Virgin is mercy only, not justice. By uniting her petitions to ours she obtains a greater quantity of grace than we could ever obtain through our weak prayers alone.

Furthermore, graces pass through Mary's hands, and, consequently, perseverance also.

Scripture affirms: "They that work by me, shall not sin. They that explain me shall have life everlasting" (Ecclus. 24:30-31).

O Mary, you entered the world without stain;
obtain for me from God
that I may leave it without sin.

St. Francis Borgia very much doubted the perseverance of those lacking a lively devotion for the
Madonna. One day while conversing with a group
of novices, he realized that many of them were
cold towards Mary. He afterwards informed the
novice master, so that he would keep a special watch
on them. It so happened that they lost their vocation
and returned to the world.

Many are conscientious about making a good
confession, but few foresee the difficulties that will
follow in overcoming new temptations.

Perseverance is real fortitude; it transforms
good acts and good dispositions into virtue. Fortitude, however, is a gift of the Holy Ghost and Mary
obtains it for souls who ask her for it.

The Church places on Mary's lips the expression: "Fortitude is mine."

As a young man, St. Andrew Corsini led a
scandalous life. His mother reprimanded him and
told him of a dream she had had before his birth
in which she had first imagined her son splendid
as an angel, than as a rapacious wolf, and, finally,
Jesus Christ's little lamb.

Andrew was converted. He went into a Church
of the Carmelites, wept at length at the feet of the
Virgin, went to confession, and requested with great
insistence to be accepted in the Carmelite Order.

From that day on Andrew, the dissolute gambler, became a model of penance: the wolf had become a lamb. He had great temptations against perseverance, especially when an uncle tried to make him leave the Carmelite Order with promises of a large inheritance and with threats. Andrew overcame all these temptations by taking refuge in Mary. Even his former friends in vice attempted to influence him many times, but, through his devotion to Mary, he not only found perseverance for himself but the conversion from wicked lives for others.

Andrew became bishop of Fiesole, an exemplar of zeal and a Saint of the Church.

Devotees of Mary are saved; those greatly devoted to Mary become Saints.

Mary is compassionate to those who wish to advance in virtue. Progress in virtue and in acquiring merit, in the vocation and in the apostolate require a continual flow of graces. It is a question of substituting Christian reasoning and principles for purely natural thinking. It is a question of placing supernatural inclinations, affections, and aspirations in the heart. It is matter of forming a supernatural will that desires poverty, purity, meekness, patience, and the like. In short, it is a question of replacing natural life with supernatural life, of making Jesus Christ dwell in us in place of egoism. It is a question of reaching the point where one can truthfully say: "It is now no longer I that live, but Christ lives in me" (Gal. 2: 20).

All this is the work of Mary. She formed Jesus Christ, considered as a true man; she received then the vocation and grace to form Jesus Christ, considered as the mystical body, that is, the faithful.

Jesus Christ was born of Mary; thus, the Madonna is the beginning of our life, that is, grace.

The Infant Jesus willed to be formed, nourished, educated, and reared by Mary. We share that happy privilege, because from her and in her the Christian is formed and grows to the fullness of age. For this reason, when Mary's duty with regard to Jesus ceased, He asked her to be a Mother to all of us.

We know through experience that pious souls devoted to Mary are more courageous in sacrifice, more prompt to obey, more modest in their behavior, and more ardent in charity; in short, they make greater spiritual progress.

The Madonna's mission is to render easy that which is difficult and arduous.

In his formula of consecration to Mary, St. Grignion de Montfort prays to her thus: "Count me among those whom you love, instruct, direct, nourish, and protect as your children and slaves. O faithful Virgin, make me a perfect disciple of Jesus Christ."

* * *

Mary is sweet to the perfect. The perfect are those who have progressed considerably in virtue. For them the name of Mary is sweetness, because after the name of Jesus, Mary is the greatest name in heaven and on earth.

The Gospel itself presents these two great and most sweet names to us: "And he called His name Jesus" (Matt. 1: 25). "And the virgin's name was Mary" (Luke 1: 27).

St. Anthony of Padua says: "The names of Jesus and Mary are joy in the heart, honey in the mouth, melody to the ear."

But here we should speak of the salutary sweetness of comfort, of love, of joy, of confidence, and of strength that Mary's name gives to those who devoutly invoke it.

In fact, the name of Mary brings freedom from temptation and it is the beginning of chastity.

The name of Mary brings courage in anxiety and in sorrow.

The name of Mary comforts the dying and fills them with hope.

St. Francis de Sales was desolate in spirit over a grave internal crisis, which had exhausted his physical and moral strength. Kneeling at the Madonna's feet, however, and consecrating himself to her, he felt himself filled with the most sublime joy, and he became the comfort of many unhappy souls.

St. Gabriel of the Sorrowful Mother found in the meditation of Mary's Dolors, the peace and joy he had once vainly sought in the dissipations of the world.

Let us belong, then, to Mary! In every age and condition of spirit let us hope in her. May the penitent, the proficient, and the perfect confide in Mary. Mary is the Mother of all.

O clement, O loving, O sweet Virgin Mary.

Hail, holy Queen, Mother of mercy, hail, our life, our sweetness, and our hope! To thee do we cry, poor banished children of Eve, to thee do we send up our sighs, mourning and weeping in this valley of tears. Turn then, most gracious advocate, thine eyes of mercy toward us; and after this our exile, show unto us the blessed fruit of thy womb, Jesus. O clement, O loving, O sweet Virgin Mary.

O Clement, O Loving. . . .

On Christmas eve, in the year 1146, St. Bernard arrived at Spira as apostolic delegate. The Saint was welcomed with extraordinary pomp. Amid the ringing of bells and singing of sacred hymns, he was led through the city to the cathedral, where the emperor and princes received him with every honor.

As the procession advanced toward the sanctuary, the choir intoned St. Bernard's favorite antiphon, the Hail Holy Queen. He was walking through the midst of an immense gathering of faithful. When the last strains of the beautiful invocation died away, after the words, "Show unto us the blessed fruit of thy womb, Jesus," Bernard, in a transport of love for Mary, made three genuflections and added, "*O clement, O loving, O sweet Virgin Mary.*"

These words, so tender and sweet, were later engraved on a bronze plate on the cathedral's floor.

Imprinting these words upon our hearts, let us often repeat as lovingly as did St. Bernard: "O clement, O loving, O sweet Virgin Mary!"

CHAPTER X

LITANY OF THE
BLESSED VIRGIN MARY

The word **litany** is derived from the Greek word, **litaneo,** meaning: I pray with insistence.

The name indicates the alternating group prayer in use since the early days of the Church.

"The Litany of the Blessed Virgin," says Bossuet, "is a series of titles of honor which the Fathers of the Church have given to Mary chiefly because of her position as Mother of God."

The Litany is composed of wondrous, golden invocations addressed to the great Mother of God.

The Litany is part of the official prayer of the Church.

The Litany of Loretto can be divided into four parts by content matter. In the first part, the person of Mary is commemorated and praised.

The second part mentions the principal Old Testament figures which refer to Mary.

The third part, beginning with "Health of the Sick," proclaims Mary's role in the world's redemption and her power on behalf of the faithful.

In the last part, the Blessed Virgin is praised for the glory she enjoys in heaven as Queen of the Universe.

It is noteworthy that from the first half of the sixteenth century it was customary at the Sanctuary of Loretto to recite a Marian litany every Saturday and on all vigils and feasts of the Blessed Virgin.

A complete text of the Litany of Loretto appeared in 1578, in a booklet written for pilgrims to the holy House of Loretto.

In 1857, Pope Sixtus V granted an indulgence for the recitation of the Litany.

More titles were later added:

December 8, 1854, Pius IX: "Queen conceived without original sin."

December 24, 1883, Leo XII: "Queen of the most holy Rosary."

April 22, 1903, Leo XIII: "Mother of good counsel."

November 16, 1915, Benedict XV: "Queen of peace."

November 1, 1950, Pius XII: "Queen assumed into heaven."

Like the other litanies, the Litany of Loretto, opens with invocations to Jesus Christ and to the three Persons of the Blessed Trinity and closes with the words of St. John the Baptist: "Lamb of God Who takes away the sin of the world!" (John 1: 29).

❉   ❉   ❉

The first part of the Litany celebrates Mary's dignity as Mother of God and the privilege of her virginity.

Holy Mary: this title recalls the eminent sanctity of Mary, who is full of the Holy Spirit, and, also, the sweetness of her name, which is the greatest after that of Jesus.

Holy Mother of God: thus, the Church expresses her faith, that is, that Jesus Christ is true God and true man, that in Him there is only one Person, that Mary is called and truly is the Mother of God.

Holy Virgin of Virgins: Mary is a virgin, but her virginity is privileged, because by her example, she attracted many souls to imitate her and because her virginity is joined to motherhood.

Mother of Christ: Mother of the Messias, the Anointed One of the Lord. Kings, priests and prophets were consecrated with oil; now, Jesus Christ is the Prophet, the eternal Priest and the supreme King.

Mother of divine grace: in fact, every grace comes through Mary from Jesus Christ; Mary is the mediatrix of grace.

Mother most pure, most chaste, inviolate and undefiled: these are four degrees of Mary's spotless purity.

Indeed, Mary was most pure of **soul,** so pure that she was disturbed at the first announcement of the Incarnation; Mary was most chaste in **body:** eyes, heart, always, everywhere; Mary was an inviolate Virgin, for God Himself willed to respect

Mother of Perpetual Help,
pray for us.

her before, during and after the Incarnation; she is called undefiled because of the splendor of her purity before the world and heaven.

Mother most amiable and most admirable, Mother of good counsel: Mary is amiable because of her incomparable spiritual and corporal beauty, which was reproduced in her Son; she is admirable, for if "God is admirable in His Saints" Mary is an abundance of wonders and merits; she is Mother of good counsel, for she is the counselor of all the doubtful.

Mother of our Creator, of our Redeemer: Mother of the Creator, because her Son Jesus Christ, as God, is the Creator of all things—"by Whom all things were made"; as Man, He is the Redeemer of the human race.

Virgin most prudent: Mary guides us through life with serene watchfulness, forseeing and providing that which is for the glory of God and our sanctification.

Virgin most venerable: to God, adoration; to Mary, supreme veneration; to the Saints, simple veneration.

Virgin most renowned: Mary must be celebrated, for she deserves the highest praise and devotion to her must be diffused among men.

Virgin most powerful: Mary's power rises from her position as Mother of God and from her very great sanctity.

Virgin most merciful: the Madonna is merciful because after that of Jesus, her heart is the most beautiful and most compassionate.

Virgin most faithful: Mary is faithful to her office of distributing grace to her most needy children, as she was faithful to her mission on earth.

Mirror of justice: justice is the sum total of all virtues; Mary possessed them all to the highest degree.

Seat of wisdom: wisdom is the first of the seven gifts of the Holy Spirit; it is the opposite of foolishness.

Cause of our joy: in Jesus, Mary is our salvation, our life and our resurrection; now, the Incarnation occurred only after Mary gave her consent to it.

Spiritual vessel, Vessel of honor: in Mary, the three theological virtues, the four cardinal virtues, the eight beatitudes, the seven gifts and the twelve fruits of the Holy Spirit are gathered, as in a precious vase.

Vessel of singular devotion: devotion is the generous will to do what divine service requires; in this disposition, Mary was the most outstanding.

✸ ✸ ✸

The second part of the Litany of the Blessed Virgin Mary recalls Old Testament symbols and figures which designated Mary.

Mystical rose: like a rose, Mary had thorns, which are the sorrowful mysteries; she had green leaves, which are the joyful mysteries of hope; she had candid petals, which are the glorious mysteries.

Tower of David: like the tower of David, Mary was strong in trials, and she is our refuge in tribulations.

Tower of ivory: ivory is highly valued and strong; "Mary, as a tower of ivory," wrote the Abbot Rupert, "is beloved by God and terrible to the devil."

House of gold: Solomon used gold profusely in the construction of his temple, in its ornaments, and in the objects of cult; Mary was adorned with every splendor, for in her the Son of God incarnate was to dwell.

Ark of the covenant: the ark contained the Tables of the Law, of the alliance between God and His people: in Mary dwelt the One Who proclaimed Himself the way, the truth and the life.

Gate of heaven: Jacob said: "This is the house of God and the gate of heaven"; all receive salvation through Mary; with the graces received through Mary, everyone can be saved.

Morning star: Mary announced the coming of the great day, in fact, the coming of the Sun of Justice, Jesus Christ.

✿   ✿   ✿

The third part of the Litany of Loretto especially recommends our needs to the Madonna.

Health of the sick: with regard to the body, poor humanity is subject to many illnesses, and Mary has compassion on us.

Refuge of sinners: ills of the soul are much more serious, and Mary reconciles sinners with God.

Comfort of the afflicted: many are the interior pains of heart and spirit, and Mary has compassion on everyone.

Help of Christians: the social needs in the Church and in civil society are many; when Mary is invoked she takes pity on all.

✿   ✿   ✿

The fourth part of the Litany exalts Mary, who was proclaimed by God Queen of heaven and earth.

Queen of angels: even the angels are surpassed in grace by Mary, and they serve her as their Queen.

Queen of patriarchs: the patriarchs were men of great virtue and particularly outstanding was their faith in the Messias; Mary, however, surpassed them all.

Queen of prophets: Mary was the subject of many prophecies and she herself prophesied great events.

Queen of apostles: Mary was the Teacher and Mother of the Apostles; she surpassed them all in zeal. She gave Jesus Christ Himself to the world.

Queen of Martyrs, Confessors, Virgins, and all Saints for three reasons: Mary gathered in herself the graces of all; she possessed them in a superior degree; she dispenses them to all the Saints.

✿   ✿   ✿

Finally:

Queen conceived without original sin: a dogma defined by Pius IX.

Queen assumed into heaven: a dogma defined by Pius XII on November 1, 1950.

Queen of the most holy Rosary: the Queen from whom Leo XIII awaited social reconstruction.

Queen of peace: during the first World War, Benedict XV wanted the world to turn to Mary, the one certain hope for peace.

O God, Who in Your mercy consecrated, through the mystery of the Incarnation of the Word, the house of the Blessed Virgin Mary and miraculously placed it in the bosom of your Church, grant that we may be separated from the society of sinners and that we may be worthy to dwell in your holy House.

The Litany on the Mountains of Abyssinia

Cardinal Massaia relates: "It was the year 1850, and I, persecuted by the heretical Bishop Salama, was taking refuge in the mountains of Abyssinia. With me were two servants and a donkey loaded with provisions; it was shortly after midnight. There was a beautiful moon that night and we saw its pale rays through the leaves of a bamboo forest. Not without fear did I hear the far-off roar of wild beasts. But trusting in Mary's protection, of which I had certain, almost visible evidence during my many years in the missions, I began to invoke her by singing the Litany. With those invocations, I felt my courage increasing and, also, my hope of escaping danger unharmed. Suddenly, however, our donkey flew into a fit of rage and the water jugs he carried crashed to the ground, along with the container of provisions. The two servants disappeared into the forest after him and I was left alone in that frightening solitude, but I continued to sing my Litany.

"Unexpectedly I heard the rustling of branches and I saw leaves moving. At first I thought a hyena was approaching, for they are very common in those parts. They rarely attack men and are little feared. Instead, however, I saw a short distance away a leopard as big as a calf with eyes like coals. In terror I glanced down and saw my bare feet. I recalled then that the sight of bare flesh enrages the beasts, and I quickly covered my feet with the sheet I had wrapped about myself. Head up, unmoving, the leopard watched me with blazing eyes. I pressed my missionary cross to my breast and prayed to the Blessed Virgin, whose praises I had sung. I begged her to save me.

"It was then that the leopard turned around and slowly withdrew. It took me a while to regain my lost wits and to continue on my way. Before long my servants met me with the donkey, again loaded with provisions, and I, after thanking the Blessed Virgin, began my journey once more."

CHAPTER XI

I WANT TO PRAISE MARY

My flowers are the fruit of honour and riches. I am the Mother of fair love, and of fear, and of knowledge, and of holy hope. In me is all grace of the way and of the truth, in me is all hope of life and of virtue (Ecclus. 24: 23-25).

My soul magnifies Mary. And my spirit rejoices in my Mother, Queen, and Teacher.

Because God has regarded the virginity and humility of His faithful handmaid: behold, heaven and earth proclaim her Mother of God.

He has done great things for Mary: she, in fact, is immaculate, virgin, assumed into heaven.

Mary's mercy is from generation to generation to all those who love and seek her.

Mary's wisdom, power, and love save the humble of heart.

Mary's goodness attracts all who regard her; all follow the perfume of her virtues.

She fills the hungry with good things; she gives light to those in darkness.

From Mary the world received Jesus Christ, blessed fruit of her womb.

In Mary Jesus Christ became for us wisdom, justice, grace, and redemption.

1) **My soul magnifies Mary.** I praise Mary with my tongue, with my hands, and with my works.

My tongue preaches Mary; my favorite, most frequent, and most ardent sermon will be the Madonna. I will not miss an occasion to speak of Mary and I will try my best to introduce this subject whenever I can. In every class I will remember that from Mary, we receive the truth: Jesus Christ. In every conversation when the opportunity arises, I will recall her mercy and privileges. I will sing of the Virgin in hymns, in vespers, and ceremonies prescribed by the Church.

My hand writes of Mary; Mary's name will head my notebooks and books. Her name will be in every article, pamphlet, and book I write.

My works will praise Mary, for I will exhibit her picture everywhere I can; I will make her the guardian and protectress of all my undertakings; I will care for altars and churches in her honor and statues, images and medals of her, spreading her devotion.

I praise Mary with my intelligence. I want to know Mary, I want to read and hear about Mary, I want to meditate on Mary. My mind will often turn to this splendid vision of heaven.

I praise Mary with my will: I wish to imitate her in her faith, in her hope, and in her charity; I wish to imitate Mary in her spirit of prayer, in her retirement and union with God; I wish to imitate Mary in her prudence and in her humility, in her private life, and in her fidelity to her mission.

I praise Mary with my heart. To Mary I give my first affections and my first thoughts on awakening; to Mary I offer frequent aspirations during the day.

2) **And my spirit rejoices in my Mother, Queen, and Teacher.** My heart rejoices in extolling my **Mother.** Jesus Christ was your true Son, O Mary. And so He wanted me to be your child, too. He is the Way and He taught it to me; He wanted to receive all from you and now it is my turn to receive all from your hands.

My spirit rejoices in extolling my **Queen.** Your kingdom is the sweetest kingdom of mercy; I make myself your subject forever.

I shall always say to you: Have pity on me, for I am the most ill, and my wounds are putrefied. Have pity on me.

My spirit rejoices in extolling my **Teacher.** You, Mary, are the holiest of creatures and model of every virtue. Imitation of Mary is easy; if I imitate the Madonna, I imitate Jesus Christ.

3) **Because God has regarded the virginity and humility of His faithful handmaid: behold, heaven and earth proclaim her Mother of God.** You are called and truly are the Mother of the Word Incarnate. A greater mother God could not have created. You bore and nourished Him Whom heaven

Holy Mary, our Lady of Deliverance, pray for us and for the holy souls in purgatory.

and earth cannot contain. Saint Elizabeth called you "Mother of God." You called Jesus with the name "Son." Jesus always honored you as His Mother and, especially does He do so now in heaven. I, too, although unworthy of pronouncing your most holy name, believe in this dogma, and with the Church I pray: "O God, Who, at the message of an angel, did will that Your Word should become incarnate in the womb of the Blessed Virgin Mary; grant to us Your servants, who believe her to be the true Mother of God, to be helped by her maternal and powerful intercession before You."

4) **He has done great things for Mary: she, in fact, is immaculate, virgin, assumed into heaven.** As you were chosen to be the Mother of God, the Lord preserved you from Eve's guilt. You were destined to bear Jesus in your womb: God sanctified His tabernacle. You were destined to form the heart of Jesus from your blood, and, therefore, He created you beautiful and full of grace.

The Lord miraculously united divine maternity with spotless virginity.

The sunset corresponds to the dawn: just as you were preserved from original sin, you were also preserved from the corruption of the grave.

5) **Mary's mercy is from generation to generation to all those who love and seek her.** Next to the heart of Jesus I hail and venerate the heart of Mary; I hope in her. This heart is my refuge and repose

in every temptation. in every sorrow, and in every hardship. I shall take shelter in your heart, O Mary, as in a safe harbor, especially at the moment of death. I await you, Mary, on my deathbed! Grant that I may call you, that I may see you, and then die in your arms. I shall always say to you: "My dear and sweet Mother Mary, keep your holy hand upon my head; guard my mind, my heart and my senses, that I be not stained with sin. Sanctify my thoughts, desires, words, and actions so that I may please you and your Jesus, my God, and reach heaven with you. Jesus and Mary, give me your holy blessing."

6) **Mary's wisdom, power, and love save the humble of heart.** You, O Mary, see our needs; you have power to help us; you are solicitous for all your children.

No one has ever called upon you in vain. All that is divided and distributed among myriads of angels and Saints is gathered in you, O Mary— everything: love, wisdom, power.

7) **Mary's goodness attracts all who regard her; all follow the perfume of her virtues.** Mary, you are good: this is what I truly want to say to you; Mary, you are merciful: this is what I would like to preach above all; Mary, you are solicitous for all: this is what I would like every sinner and every needy person to know.

8) **She has filled the hungry with good things; she gives light to those in darkness.** May Mary be praised on every shore and in every desert, on every mountain and on every sea, in every city and in every countryside, in heaven, and on earth. May men write of Mary in prose and poetry; may music sing of Mary and paintbrushes labor for Mary: may sculptors erect monuments to Mary and architects work for her; may monarchs bow to Mary and nations have recourse to her.

May science, philosophy, and theology serve Mary, as well as motion pictures, radio, television, and the press.

9) **From Mary the world received Jesus Christ, blessed fruit of her womb.** This Rod bore the flower, Jesus Christ: the light of the world. Mary presented Him to the shepherds and to the Magi; she presented Him in the Temple and to the Apostles. She gave Him to the whole world, in a better way than any apostle did: she is the Queen of Apostles. She is the Virgin whose Son is Christ (St. Jerome), the Vessel of divinity (St. Bernard), the Throne of Christ the Pontiff (St. Athanasius), the Soil which produces the Savior (St. Ildefonsus), the Undefiled Temple in which dwells the Word of God (St. Epiphanius).

10) **In Mary Jesus Christ became for us wisdom, justice, grace, and redemption.** Everything came from Jesus through Mary. At her appearance

the Old Testament closed and the New began. Satan felt his kingdom trembling and saw the kingdom of Jesus Christ advancing. Heaven and earth exchanged the kiss of peace. The darkness of paganism became less dense. Virtue and love were born and began to grow on earth. Idolatry retreated; God began to be adored in spirit and truth; a new glory was given to God and new peace to the world. Slaves were liberated, tyrants defeated, families restored. A new order arose, a new philosophy, a new theology. Behold, everything was renewed! For God the Father wanted everything restored in His Son—everything: all that is in heaven as well as all that is on earth.

You are the urn containing God (John Geom.); you are the urn of heavenly manna (St. Thomas Aquinas), most fertile Vine of truth (St. Epiphanius); Vine that bears the vine of the Church—Christ (St. Andrew Corsini).

My soul praises Mary and Mary praises God. Mary attributes all her greatness to the Lord; to the Blessed Trinity she gives every honor, praise, virtue, thanksgiving, love, and adoration for all eternity.

Mary praises God and I unite myself to her: through Mary, with Mary, and in Mary I sing to God.

My soul magnifies the Lord and my spirit rejoices in God my Savior; because He has regarded the lowliness of His handmaid: for, behold, henceforth, all generations shall call me blessed, because He Who is mighty has done great things for me.

O my Lady, Mary, take me under your blessed protection and special guardianship, in the bosom of your mercy. I recommend to you my soul and body today, always, and at the hour of my death; to you I confide every hope and consolation, every anxiety and misery, my life and my death, so that through your holy intercession and merits, all my works may be regulated and ordered according to the will of your Son and your will. Amen.

The Remembrance of a Dying Mother

A poor widow lived in Paris with her only son who was her sole happiness. Her deceased husband had left her in dire poverty. Because of her sorrow over the loss of her husband, added to her sacrifices and lack of food, the good mother became critically ill.

When the end was near, she called to her bedside her son, Hubald, who was not yet eighteen. "Hubald," she said, "I am about to die; I want to make my last will."

"And what will can you make now that we are in such deplorable poverty?" asked the son.

"This is what I leave you: put your hand under my pillow, and you will find the treasure." Hubald searched and found a rosary. "This is what I leave you, my son; I possess nothing else, but I leave you enough. In memory of your poor mother, remember to recite it every day." With tears in his eyes Hubald promised his mother never to go a day without saying it. Left alone in the world and penniless, he joined the armed forces and was sent to Crimea.

Before long he attained high military rank and, at the age of thirty, became a colonel. Gradually, however, Hubald lost every religious sentiment.

Nevertheless, he kept the promise made to his mother and never failed to recite the rosary. While reciting it, he would think to himself: "What a state I am in! O my poor mother, if you only knew what has become of me! I recite the rosary but I have no more religion. My soul is full of sins." While he was one evening reflecting in this manner, rosary in hand, he felt a tap on his shoulder and heard, "Colonel, are you still awake?" Hubald turned and saw that it was the army chaplain; he gave him his hand and the chaplain felt the rosary beads. "Oh, you still say the rosary, Colonel? I am glad; I did not think you were so devout."

Hubald then told the whole story of his mother.

The chaplain took advantage of the deep emotion of the moment to win him over. He comforted him by explaining that God was so good as to pardon all his sins. He encouraged him to go to confession, assuring him that he would thus find peace and serenity of heart.

God's grace worked. With tears in his eyes, the colonel made a general confession. The joy he experienced was indescribable. Within a few moments, trumpets sounded, and the cry: "To arms!" echoed on all sides. The enemy was attacking. The colonel arose, assembled his troops, and marched against the enemy. At the walls of Malakoff, a fierce battle ensued. Soldiers were falling on all sides. A few hours later, the French army gained the victory.

When the battle was over, however, it was found that the colonel had been struck by a bullet and had expired on the field of valor. The rosary had opened heaven to him.

VARIOUS PRAYERS TO
THE BLESSED VIRGIN MARY

Our Lady, Help of Christians

Immaculate Virgin, Mother of God and our Mother, Mary, thou seest the attacks that are everywhere made by the devil and the world upon the Catholic faith, in which, by God's grace, we intend to live and die, in order that we may attain to eternal glory. Do thou, the Help of Christians, renew thine ancient victories and save thy children. They entrust to thee their firm purpose never to enroll themselves in societies hostile to our holy religion; do thou, who art all holy, present to thy divine Son our good resolutions and obtain for us the grace we need to be unshaken in their observance even to the end of life. Console the visible Head of the Church, sustain the Catholic episcopate, protect the clergy and people who proclaim thee Queen; by the power of thine intercession hasten the day when all nations shall be gathered at the feet of the chief Shepherd. Amen.

Mary, Help of Christians, pray for us!

* * *

Our Lady, Queen of Peace

Most holy Virgin, Mother of God and our most loving Mother, by thy divine maternity thou didst merit to share in thy divine Son's prerogative of universal kingship; we, thy most humble servants and devoted children, feel ourselves comforted by the thought that, as it pleased the Redeemer of mankind to have Himself announced by the Prophets and by the Angels at Bethlehem under the glorious title of King of Peace, so too it must be pleasing to thee to hear thyself saluted and honored by us under the title of Queen of Peace, a title that is so dear to thy motherly heart; it is an invocation poured forth with great fervor from our hearts. May thy powerful intercession ward off from thy people all hatred and discord, and direct their hearts in the ways of peace and brotherhood, which Jesus Christ came to teach and enforce among men for the prosperity and safety of all, and in which paths Holy Church does not cease to guide our steps. Vouchsafe, O glorious Queen, to regard with kindly eyes and to crown with success the paternal solicitude, wherewith the Sovereign Pontiff, the Vicar on earth of thy divine Son, continually seeks to call together and unite the nations about the only center of saving Faith; grant that to us also in filial submission to our common Father, it may be given to correspond wholeheartedly with his salutary designs. Enlighten the rulers of our country as to those same designs; quicken and maintain peace and concord in our families, peace in our hearts and Christian charity throughout all the world. Amen.

❖   ❖   ❖

Our Lady of the Sacred Heart

Remember, Our Lady of the Sacred Heart, what ineffable power thy divine Son hath given thee over His own adorable Heart. Filled with confidence in thy merits, we come before thee and implore thy protection. O heavenly Treasurer of the Heart of Jesus, that Heart which is the inexhaustible source of all graces, which thou mayest open to us at thy good pleasure, in order that from it may flow forth upon mankind the riches of love and mercy, light and salvation, that are contained therein; grant unto us, we beseech thee, the favors which we seek.... We can never, never be refused by thee, and since thou art our Mother, O Our Lady of the Sacred Heart, graciously receive our prayers and grant our request. Amen.

✿   ✿   ✿

Our Lady of Intercession

Most Holy Mary, Our Lady of Intercession, whose maternal tenderness gathers in one embrace all the souls redeemed by the Precious Blood of thy Son Jesus, we come before thy royal throne with sadness in our hearts as we remember those who have gone before us, but also with unlimited confidence in thine intercession. Death, which burst asunder the bonds of earth, has not destroyed the affection which binds us to those who lived in the same faith we do. O Mary, countless souls await with unutterable anxiety the assistance of our prayers, and the merits of our good works in that place of expiation. Urged by the charity of Jesus Christ, we raise our countenance and heart in supplication to thee, the compassionate Mother of all believers, in favor of those suffering souls. Make our prayers of good effect, O Mary; obtain for them the power to move the Heart of Jesus our Redeemer through thy motherly intercession. Let thine incomparable holiness supply the defects of our misery, thy love make good our languid affection, thy power strengthen our weakness. Grant, O Queen of heaven, that the ardent desire of the souls of the departed to be admitted to the Beatific Vision may soon be satisfied. We pray to thee, O Mother, especially for the souls of our relations, of priests, of those who were zealous in honoring thee, of those who did good to the souls of others, of those who wept with them and for them and, finally, for the souls of those who are forgotten. Grant that one day, when we are all reunited in heaven, we may be able to rejoice in the possession of God, in the happiness of thy dear presence, in the fellowship of all the Saints, thanking thee forever for all the blessings thou hast obtained for us, O Mother, who art our unfailing comfort. Amen.

Hail Mary *three times,* and *once* Eternal rest grant unto them, *etc.*

❋   ❋   ❋

Our Lady of the Rosary

Queen of the most holy Rosary, in these times of such brazen impiety, manifest thy power with the signs of thine ancient victories, and from thy throne, whence thou dost dispense pardon and graces, mercifully regard the Church of thy Son, His Vicar on earth, and every order of clergy and laity, who are sore oppressed in the mighty conflict. Do thou, who art the powerful vanquisher of all heresies, hasten the hour of mercy, even though the hour of God's justice is every day provoked by the countless sins of men. For me who am the least of men, kneeling before thee in supplication, do thou obtain the grace I need to live righteously upon earth and to reign among the just in heaven, the while in company with all faithful Christians throughout the world, I salute thee and acclaim thee as Queen of the most holy Rosary:

Queen of the most holy Rosary, pray for us.

✿   ✿   ✿

Our Lady of Good Counsel

Most glorious Virgin, chosen by the eternal Counsel to be the Mother of the eternal Word made flesh, thou who art the treasurer of divine graces and the advocate of sinners, I who am thy most unworthy servant have recourse to thee; be thou pleased to be my guide and counselor in this vale of tears. Obtain for me through the Most Precious Blood of thy divine Son, the forgiveness of my sins, the salvation of my soul and the means necessary to obtain it. In like manner obtain for Holy Church victory over her enemies and the spread of the kingdom of Jesus Christ upon the whole earth. Amen.

Daughters of St. Paul

IN MASSACHUSETTS
    50 St. Paul's Ave., Jamaica Plain, Boston, MA 02130;
      617-522-8911; 617-522-0875
    172 Tremont Street, Boston, MA 02111; **617-426-5464;**
      617-426-4230
IN NEW YORK
    78 Fort Place, Staten Island, NY 10301; **212-447-5071**
    59 East 43rd Street, New York, NY 10017; **212-986-7580**
    625 East 187th Street, Bronx, NY 10458; **212-584-0440**
    525 Main Street, Buffalo, NY 14203; **716-847-6044**
IN NEW JERSEY
    Hudson Mall — Route 440 and Communipaw Ave.,
      Jersey City, NJ 07304; **201-433-7740**
IN CONNECTICUT
    202 Fairfield Ave., Bridgeport, CT 06604; **203-335-9913**
IN OHIO
    2105 Ontario St. (at Prospect Ave.), Cleveland, OH 44115; **216-621-9427**
    25 E. Eighth Street, Cincinnati, OH 45202; **513-721-4838**
IN PENNSYLVANIA
    1719 Chestnut Street, Philadelphia, PA 19103; **215-568-2638**
IN VIRGINIA
    1025 King St., Alexandria, VA 22314
IN FLORIDA
    2700 Biscayne Blvd., Miami, FL 33137; **305-573-1618**
IN LOUISIANA
    4403 Veterans Memorial Blvd., Metairie, LA 70002; **504-887-7631;**
      504-887-0113
    1800 South Acadian Thruway, P.O. Box 2028, Baton Rouge, LA 70821
      504-343-4057; 504-343-3814
IN MISSOURI
    1001 Pine Street (at North 10th), St. Louis, MO 63101; **314-621-0346;**
      314-231-1034
IN ILLINOIS
    172 North Michigan Ave., Chicago, IL 60601; **312-346-4228**
      312-346-3240
IN TEXAS
    114 Main Plaza, San Antonio, TX 78205; **512-224-8101**
IN CALIFORNIA
    1570 Fifth Avenue, San Diego, CA 92101; **714-232-1442**
    46 Geary Street, San Francisco, CA 94108; **415-781-5180**
IN HAWAII
    1143 Bishop Street, Honolulu, HI 96813; **808-521-2731**
IN ALASKA
    750 West 5th Avenue, Anchorage AK 99501; **907-272-8183**
IN CANADA
    3022 Dufferin Street, Toronto 395, Ontario, Canada
IN ENGLAND
    128, Notting Hill Gate, London W11 3QG, England
    133 Corporation Street, Birmingham B4 6PH, England
    5A-7 Royal Exchange Square, Glasgow G1 3AH, England
    82 Bold Street, Liverpool L1 4HR, England
IN AUSTRALIA
    58 Abbotsford Rd., Homebush, N.S.W.,   2140, Australia